ME, MY GUITAR, & NINA SIMONE

ME, MY GUITAR, & NINA SIMONE

Stories of My Musical Life and Adventures with Nina

43 Amazing Years As Her Guitarist, Music Director, and Confidant

AL SCHACKMAN

A.G. DUNEWOOD PUBLISHING CO. | WAGON MOUND, NM

Published by
A.G. Dunewood Publishing Co. LLC | Wagon Mound, NM

Publisher's Cataloging-in-Publication Data
Schackman, Al.

Me, my guitar, and Nina Simone : stories of my musical life and adventures with Nina : 43 years as her guitarist, music director, and confidant
Al Schackman – Wagon Mound, NM :
A.G. Dunewood Publishing Co. LLC, 2026.

p. ; cm.

ISBN13: 978-0-9601319-0-7

1. Schackman, Al. 2. Guitarists--United States--Biography.
3. Simone, Nina--1933-2003.

ML418.S33 M46 2025
787.2092--dc23

Project coordination by Jenkins Group, Inc.
www.jenkinsgroupinc.com

Interior design by Christine Kettner

Printed in the United States of America
30 29 28 27 26 • 5 4 3 2 1

To my children: Aurin, Steffan, Davi, and Kris.
How lucky I am to be loved by you.

FOR GINNY
who brought me to her oasis and
might not know how deeply I cherish her.

CONTENTS

INTRODUCTION

Nina Simone. What path would my life have taken without our lives colliding? At the age of ninety-two, I have been a professional musician for seventy-five years, forty-three of them as Nina's guitarist, as well as her close friend. Playing with Nina, especially just the two of us alone, was often a soaring and extraordinary experience. Sometimes, in dreams, I can hear us, hear her, and at times, the two of us playing on a song we never played together. I just knew her so well that even our dreams collided. As her friend, that entanglement continued, as I was challenged to support her difficult psychological problems.

I was literally lucky to be able to make a living playing my guitar. So many brilliant musicians never get the right breaks, and go on to other careers. As a teenager, I was spurred along by a wonderful teacher and mentor, Rector Baily, and met another of his students, bassist Chris White, who became my close friend, later playing with Nina also, and then with Dizzy Gillespie for many years. I was drafted during the Korean War and ended up in Special Services, playing in a band with fellow draftees Wynton Kelly and Duke Pearson, and even accompanying country star, "Corporal" Faron Young. I then returned to New York in the 1950s, when jazz and R&B guitarists were in demand, and with my various connections, I was able to work full time. Then, in the summer of 1958, I met Nina.

As my career wove in and out with Nina's, I was also able to work with many other notable people. I played with Harry Belafonte for five years and consequently toured with Martin Luther King during the Civil Rights Movement.

Over the years, I have recounted many of my life's adventures to family and friends and have been urged to put them in a book. Some are hilarious, and some are even historically relevant today. My stories of Nina Simone are intimate and revealing, stories only someone so closely involved with her can bring to the reader. I also describe the dangers encountered when traveling with Martin Luther King, together with harrowing experiences as a white musician traveling with a Black band in the segregated South. The stories that follow are also about various encounters with celebrities as well as world travels. It's a long look back, but, speaking of lucky, at ninety-two, my adventures are still rolling on.

—Al Schackman
Wagon Mound, New Mexico, 2025

PLAY IT AGAIN SAM

As Nina Simone's guitarist,
there were times that Nina performed
engagements without her band, just the two of us.
This one is memorable.

IT WAS THREE in the morning when the phone rang. "Al, I want you to meet me in Morocco in three days. The Idou Anfa hotel in Casablanca is opening an exclusive skyline music room and naming it the Nina Simone Lounge in my honor. They are covering my fee, all expenses, and, of course, you'll be paid handsomely. It will be fabulous, just you and me. We don't need anyone else to get in our way." *Ohhhkaayy,* this was Nina on the phone calling from Switzerland to my farm in Massachusetts. The seductress, the siren luring my ship onto the rocks. Not the first time for these nocturnal events. "Al, I presumed you would be on board and took the liberty of having the Moroccan people book you a round-trip ticket, which will be held for you at the Royal Air Maroc desk at JFK."

"Whoa, Nina, back up a minute. Don't I need a visa?"

"No," she said, "are you forgetting who I am? I played a command solo performance at a birthday party for King Hassan the Second's daughter, Princess Lalla Meryem, at the royal palace two years ago, and was assured that your visa will be waived, so you'd better be there. We will be treated royally."

Hold on tight, Alvin. As I remember it, that command performance was a little bumpy and I'm surprised that Nina is being invited back. I asked Nina about that incident, and she fluffed it off.

"Just a misunderstanding about certain customs," she said. "It was smoothed over."

As I had heard it, Nina took off her clothes and dove into the royal pool, not an unusual event for her. Morocco was a modern-leaning but still conservative country. King Hassan was bringing his people toward a forward-thinking society and although a Muslim country, Morocco maintained cordial relations with the Israeli government and was host to a thriving local Jewish community, but there were still limits to its openness.

"Okay, Nina, but I need at least four days."

"Wrong, Al. You have tomorrow to get yourself ready, the next day get yourself down to JFK; the flight is that night and you arrive the next day. You have plenty of time. Three days is all you need. See you there."

"But Nina . . . Nina?"

She had hung up the phone.

Oh boy, here we go again on another Nina adventure. Or misadventure? I asked myself, *why? Why do I allow myself to fall into her spell?* And she did hold a spell over me. Of course, there was the music, especially when it was just her and me alone. Nothing came close to the magic we created together. Also, she was at times like a little sister who needed to be looked after, mischievous but innocent and vulnerable, attracting undesirable elements looking to take advantage of her. There was also her violent shadow side, where I always needed to be on guard in order to divert her from very serious repercussions.

I wondered why she had waited until the last minute to call me. She must have known about this for a while. Maybe she was going to do the engagement alone but then thought it better to have me with her, for the music, companionship, and probably as a security blanket. But indeed, there was a nonstop, first-class, round-trip ticket waiting for me at the JFK Royal Air Maroc counter with a Moroccan government visa waiver attached. I was hooked.

The flight left in the evening, was uneventful, and I landed at Mohammed V International Airport the next morning. There was a very nice English-speaking lady waiting to meet me with a sign reading, "Hello Mr. Shachmann." I've had my name spelled every which way and would have to add this one to the list. She introduced herself as Yolanda, a friend and associate of Mr. Habbibi, the hotel manager. We arrived at the hotel, and I was cordially greeted by Mr. Habbibi, a very charming gentleman, excited about hosting what was to be "the" social event of the year. I was taken to my room, a quite comfortable junior suite. I went down to the bar and thought to myself that this whole scene was very upscale and continental, with posters of Humphrey Bogart and Ingrid Bergman from the movie *Casablanca* hanging on the walls. It was not unlike my experiences when playing with Nina in Juan les Pins on the French Riviera, or Montreux in Switzerland. Maybe this would work out with no ripples after all.

As I was settling in, the phone rang in my room. It was Mr. Habbibi asking if the accommodations were to my satisfaction and eager to show me the Nina Simone Room. I met him in the lobby, and up we went to the roof. The elevator opened to a beautiful room with a panoramic 360-degree view of the city, and was laid out like a little Greek amphitheater with a white grand piano down in the center. Sofas and lounge chairs were on different tiers rising up around the room. Quite elegant, Nina was going to love this. I tried the piano, which I found to be nicely in tune, and also noticed a Fender Twin Reverb guitar amp sitting nearby. They hadn't missed a trick. I expressed to Mr. Habibi how impressed I was with the care they were taking to make sure that Miss Simone would be happy. He was going to meet Nina as soon as she arrived and had invited us to dinner that evening.

Meanwhile, as all these pleasantries were going on, Nina's flight arrived from Switzerland, where she had been staying with a very wealthy woman, Suzanne Baumann, and her partner, who evidently were going to promote a series of concerts for her. Yolanda, that very nice woman who met me at the airport, also met Nina there, and shakenly related this story to me.

"Al, I met Nina's flight with a bouquet of flowers, put her in the limo, gathered her bags, and headed into the city. Nina ordered me to immediately take her to police headquarters. I asked what was wrong, and she said I would soon find out as I would be her interpreter. I directed the driver to the main headquarters of the National Police, where she got out and yelled, 'C'MON, and you just translate exactly what I say.' In we went and up to the front desk. Nina went into her bag, pulled out a revolver, slammed it on the desk, and in English said, 'I am Nina Simone. There are two lesbians after me that want to kill me, and I need protection.'

"Al, I translated exactly. They immediately called in one of their senior officers, who spoke English, who then listened to her relate how these two women in Switzerland were trying to enslave her and make her play concerts. The officer asked where she got the gun and how was she able to bring it into the country? She replied that she was an international star and therefore not subjected to being searched. I told the officer that she was here with the government's blessing. He picked up the phone, spoke to someone and then said, 'Welcome to Morocco, Miss Simone. You are now under our protection and will not need your firearm. We will be on the lookout for these women.' Nina was then very cordial to him, thanked him as he escorted us back to the limousine, and invited him to her performance. Mr. Schackman, this is exactly what happened. Is Nina going to be alright?"

Oh lord, I said to myself. *Is this a portent of things to come?*

Time to greet Nina. I rang the buzzer to her suite. A young woman, who must have been tasked with attending to her, opened the door and said, "You must be Mr. Schackman. Madame Simone told me you would probably be arriving shortly and to show you to her bedroom."

I entered a lavishly decorated setting that could have been straight out of Scheherazade. Gilded appointments on furniture and a silk-canopied bed so large I could hardly see Nina sitting up in it.

"DAHHHLING," she cried, threw down a fashion magazine,

held out her arms and said, "Come on over here and give Nina a big smooch." This was a ritual we performed throughout our relationship when I would join her somewhere or other in the world, almost always with her in bed. Can't say I didn't love the feeling. In *those* moments, she was her real, sincere, essential self, so much fun, so lovely, and I just basked in her presence. All well and good, but I reminded myself of the story Yolanda had shared with me earlier.

"How was your flight?" I asked.

"Oh, the flight was fine, but Switzerland was a drag. A very wealthy Swiss lesbian and her lover wanted to manage me and book concerts. They drew up a contract and offered me a 20,000-dollar signing bonus. I said, 'Let me see the money.' Christine had a certified bank check drawn up and delivered it to me. So I signed, Al, signed in good faith. Of course, I was a fool and didn't read the contract first. I had the twenty grand and just signed my name. When I looked, it said that the money was an advance, not a signing bonus. I went ballistic. They said they never said it was a bonus; it was an advance. Well, I kept my cool, went to the bank and cashed it for US dollars, got on my flight to Casablanca, and VOILA! Here I am with the money. They shouldn't have messed with Nina. Enough of that, let's have some champagne!"

That was quite a story, but it is just a prelude of what was about to unfold.

That evening, we arrived at the hotel restaurant for dinner hosted by Mr. Habbibi, whom I learned was not only the executive director of the hotel but also a member of the Moroccan Council of the Arts, a government agency that was sponsoring this event. Also in attendance was Yolanda and the director of the arts council, his wife, and the publisher of the national newspaper and his wife. Everyone was fluent in English. Champagne was served. The menu had been prearranged by Mr. Habbibi, who said it would be a nouveau-style dinner of traditional Moroccan cuisine.

Nina was pleasant until, unfortunately, one of the women spoke up to ask about Nina's flight. Nina immediately went into describing the whole story of her "escape" from Switzerland and subsequent events at the police station. She didn't miss a beat and included that very cute police officer she had invited to the concert and suggested that he be assigned to her as security throughout her stay. Mr. Habbibi fielded that beautifully, saying that security was completely taken care of, but Nina insisted on that officer, and Mr. Habbibi replied that he would see what he could do. Dinner progressed without further ado. Nina enjoyed her food, ordered a brandy, and with a "Come, Al, see me to my suite," rose and said good night. I was invited to rejoin the group when Nina was settled in for the night, which I did. I knew full well that I would have to watch what I said for the rest of the evening, and I was right, as there was much concern about Nina when I returned.

The next morning, Yolanda phoned and asked if I thought Nina would like to come to her house for a quiet lunch. She had a young friend, a well-known fashion photographer and a big fan of Nina's, who would love to meet her. I went to Nina's room, and she was in bed having breakfast. I was surprised when she said she would be delighted to meet this young man. She then went on to tell me that she wanted me to go with her for a day trip over to Gibraltar, where Jean-Luc Young, the head of Charly Records, was staying, to demand the royalties from her recording of "My Baby Just Cares for Me," which she claimed he had pirated. This was an area of business from which I always tried to distance myself. I left that to Nina and her agent, Raymond Gonzalez, but he wasn't in on this deal. I told her I should stay in Casablanca to finish up any payment details with Mr. Habbibi, and she agreed.

That afternoon, we went to Yolanda's, met her photographer friend, and Nina charmed him to death. We had a lovely lunch, and the photographer told Nina he would be honored to do some fashion shoots with her as a gift if she would like that. Nina jumped at it and invited the young man to accompany her to Gibraltar the day after the concert, saying that they could take photos along the way and have an enjoyable day.

She just had one little business thing she had to take care of there, and she would spring for the airfare. The guy was enraptured and captured. Yolanda said she would arrange the flights, saying it was a short flight, quickly connecting in Spain with a commuter hop to Gibraltar.

I was off the hook.

In the early evening, Mr. Habbibi phoned up and was very excited about the performance. The room was already filling up, and he asked how Nina was feeling. I told him she was getting dressed and all was well. Actually, she was in her bathrobe smoking and drinking champagne, while going on about Suzanne Baumann and Jean-Luc Young, working herself up, and not wanting to focus with me on working up the set list for the evening. She said we would just wing it as this wasn't a real concert, just a club in a "third world" country. *Oh boy, here we go.* I thought she was morphing into that space where I couldn't find my friend, my sister. Here was somebody who earlier had been delighted to be attending this dedication honoring her and getting paid handsomely to do so. By now, she should have been dressed, but she was walking around in her bathrobe with her voice becoming louder and angrier.

I need to say that throughout the years her behavior was talked about in the press and in reviews. "She was drunk," they would say, was "on drugs," or "just mean," etc, etc . . . The reality was that Nina had a serious bipolar condition, not fully understood back then, which I will get into more fully later.

So, there we were, with me trying to steer her on. We were to start at nine, and it was fast approaching. She went into the bedroom with the young assistant while I waited . . . and waited. Eventually, the girl came out very scared and said Madame Simone was on the phone, yelling at someone. No kidding. You could probably hear it in the hallway. It was 9:30, and the doorbell rang. It was Mr. Habbibi, very nervous, very wanting to know if there was a problem. I told him Nina had some difficulty with her outfit, and we would be there shortly. He left, and I went into the bedroom, and voila, Nina was dressed. She said she had been on the phone trying to get Jean-Luc's private phone number, and "Now let's go get this damn thing over with."

"Well, at least the room is nice enough to have my name on it," Nina whispered as I escorted her down the steps to the piano. She dropped her bag by her side, and I strapped on my guitar. She looked at the set list I had prepared on my own, looked at me angrily and said, "I thought I told you I wouldn't need a set list." Then into the microphone, "You're lucky I'm here. I don't play clubs and lounges anymore. You've finally allowed black people to appear in concert halls, and I don't have to play these bars anymore."

Hang on, Alvin, I said to myself, *we're back in the Twilight Zone.*

Nina then went on about Charly Records. She was into the whole nine yards, and the audience had no idea what she was going on about. They had been patiently waiting for what must have been an hour and a half, and suddenly a woman interrupted Nina and said in eloquent English, "Nina, we are all here because we love your music and are shocked at your rude and disrespectful behavior toward other human beings. What is wrong with you that makes you so disdainful of others? Since you are obviously not going to perform, I'm sad for you, but I don't need to sit here and listen to your ranting." With that said, she rose from her chair and started up the stairs to the elevator.

Nina yelled, "YOU BITCH," and in a flash reached into her bag, pulled out a knife, unsheathed it, yes, unsheathed the thing, this was no pocketknife, and took off up the stairs after the woman. I quickly unstrapped my guitar and chased up the stairs after Nina with the crowd frozen in place at this unfolding drama. The woman reached the elevator, Nina reached the landing, and the woman saw Nina with the knife and was terrified. I reached Nina and grabbed her from behind. The elevator door opened, and I yelled to the woman, "GET IN!" She did, and the elevator closed just in time because I couldn't hold on to Nina much longer, as she had enormous strength. I pushed the button for the other elevator, the doors opened, and I hustled Nina in and pushed her floor. Down we went with Nina screaming at me for interfering. "Did you hear what she said to me? You expect me to sit there and let that bitch get away with that? Nobody talks to Nina Fucking Simone like that and gets away with it." We reached her floor. I got her into the room and told the girl to look after her while I went back to retrieve Nina's things. As I was closing the door, Nina laughed and said, "At least we didn't have to do the show."

I went back up and the room was still full, and people were talking about the scene Nina put on. I went to the piano, sat down, apologized for Nina's behavior, and was barraged with questions. It was like a press conference. People raised their hands asking questions. The back-and-forth went on for a while. I just felt obligated, so I sat there at the piano and played, and eventually the crowd filtered out.

Mr. Habbibi came up to me and said, "Al, do you often have to deal with Nina being this way?"

I said, "No, not very often, but it does occur from time to time. It's a serious condition we have to deal with. I'm so sorry it happened here."

He told me that the woman who reprimanded Nina was the wife of a government minister and the publisher of the foremost Middle East fashion magazine. He shook his head, said Nina was lucky to have a friend like me with her, and asked if I would meet with him at his office in the morning to discuss things. I knew where that was going to go.

The next morning, I sat down with him, and while he sympathized with Nina's condition, the hotel refunded the guests, suffered a public embarrassment, and was not going to pay her. I went to Nina and gave her the news. She took it quietly, said she was about to leave for Gibraltar with the photographer, and would deal with it when she got back. Here I was in Casablanca, and my flight out was not until after the weekend. I'd have to speak with Mr. Habbibi about my room.

An hour later, Mr. Habbibi phoned up and frantically asked me to come right down to his office. Nina had barged in while he was away, demanded to see him and be paid. His secretary said he was out, and Nina proceeded to tear up the office, throwing things around and then storming out.

I walked in and, oh my, what a mess. We just looked at each other. Over a cup of coffee, Mr. Habbibi said that Nina's suite was to be vacated that day. Yolanda would help pack her things and would store them until further instructions. He then surprised me by saying the hotel would appreciate me staying on through the weekend as their guest, and if I would play through the weekend, the hotel would pay my fee. I agreed but wondered, when the time came, how I was going to deal with Nina.

Well, I never had to deal with her. That night, the photographer showed up at the hotel looking for me. "What are you doing back?" I asked. He told me that they had arrived in Gibraltar and Nina was treating him like a servant, ordering him to do this and that. She told him to phone Jean-Luc Young of Charly Records. There was repeatedly no answer, and she was extremely angry. They went to lunch, and she then asked him to go with her to the police to see if they could locate Jean-Luc. They found the police bureau, went through the whole "I'm

Nina Simone" story to an English-speaking person who went through some directories and told them there was no one by that name listed on Gibraltar.

By that point, it was time to catch the last flight back. The photo shoot was down the tubes. They went to the airport for their flight to Spain and connection back to Casablanca. In Spain, Nina showed her passport, whereupon an officer checked it and said he had an order from the Moroccan government that Nina Simone was denied permission to enter Morocco. Nina was furious. The photographer was already on the other side of passport control and was not allowed to go back. He said the last he saw of her before getting on the plane . . . she was sitting on a bench waiting to speak with the American consulate.

Adventures with Nina. Will I never learn?

BACKGROUND MUSIC

So . . . how did my life lead me to Casablanca
with the brilliant Nina Simone?
It was a long adventure.

I GUESS I WAS geared up for music early on. I was told that when I was around a year and a half old, I was singing "Home on the Range" and "Little Sir Echo, How Do You Do," holding my ear out to listen for the echo, someone singing back "hello, hello." I don't remember that but I do remember when I was four visiting my Gramma Esther, (my mother's mom), in Brooklyn, and being fascinated by men carrying huge blocks of ice up many flights of tenement stairs for the ice box in peoples' apartments, and the mysterious junk man on his horse-drawn wagon driving down the street yelling in a sing-song voice "Rags ol' Iron, Rags ol' Iron," the old cowbells strung across the wagon jingling with the rhythm of the horse clippity clopping along. Ironic that years later, as a young guitarist with Nina Simone, she would sing "Rags ol' Iron," a song by Oscar Brown Jr., with me imitating the sound of them old cowbells on the guitar.

In 1940, when I was seven, my brother David was born, and we went out to visit Dad's family on the Empire State Express streamliner. My grandparents had immigrated from Russia around 1910 and were living in Cleveland after leaving their farm in central Ohio a few years earlier. Gramps was one tough old bird, now in the salvage business, meaning he had a horse named Brownie and a junk wagon, making the rounds of factories for scrap copper and iron. He would take me with him, sitting me up on the seat and letting me hold the reins. I was in heaven. We'd pull over for lunch, and Gramps would put a feed bag on Brownie, open the lunch box Gramma had prepared, hand me a sandwich and a mason jar of chocolate milk. He sipped on his jar of vodka that mysteriously appeared, after having already downed a glass of schnapps before leaving the house, and he would expound on life and the sorry state of the war in Europe. Yeah, he could put away the vodka like a champ and never show it, something I had to think about later on in my own life.

My parents were living on a farm in the Catskill Mountains seven miles outside of Monticello, NY, and about a mile west of Sackett Lake, where in the summer I would troll at night for largemouth bass in my dad's rowboat while listening to the hot Latin bands of Tito Rodriguez, Machito, Tito Puente, or Noro Morales that played in the Laurels Country Club Hotel's riverboat casino perched on the edge of the lake. I would hear Rodriguez's band singing out "Donde, Donde Estabas Tu," and sing along. I later learned it meant "where were you." I guess the girl in the song stood him up, but not me . . . I was right there sitting in the boat offshore in the dark, soaking it all in. No better way to learn Latin music.

I was a hardworking kid, I thought, bringing in the cows from pasture for milking, morning and evening, and then helping to strip out the milk by hand after they were on the milking machines. We milked thirty-five cows, mostly Holsteins with a few Jerseys and Guernseys, in a barn built in the seventeen hundreds with pegged hand-hewn timbers by the English ancestors of Howard Pelton, the farmer next door, who was semi-retired and enjoying his fox hunting in the winter and sugaring his maple stand in the spring. He kept three foxhounds that were named Mike, Joe, and Tom, and when one died, another would take its place and receive the old one's name. That held true for the draft horses as well. Mike, Joe, and Tom. Simplicity fine-tuned.

I have never lost my love for rural life. The values, honesty, and integrity that it encompasses would stay with me, and also help maintain my equilibrium as I worked my way through my adult years.

MOVING TO BROOKLYN

WHEN WORLD WAR II was just ending, and I was going on twelve years old, we had moved from the farm to Passaic, New Jersey, where my dad was working in a defense plant. We then moved to Brooklyn. To me, it felt like I had been dumped onto a prehistoric planet, but instead of dinosaurs, I ran into the neighborhood guys, an unruly bunch of raptors calling themselves The Jesters Social Athletic Club. They found out about the new kid on the block and started ringing the doorbell for the top-floor apartment of the Eastern Parkway brownstone where we lived. I don't know how they found out my name, but one Monday, they yelled up after dinner, asking if Alvin, not Al as I preferred to be called, could come down and play. My mother was so happy I was making friends. *Sure, Mom!* What was really going on . . . I was taken down to Lincoln Terrace Park with them each evening for a boxing match to see where they would place me in their pecking order. My dad had been an excellent amateur boxer in his youth in Cleveland and had taught me some of boxing's finer points. I could take care of business, having redeemed myself fairly well in a couple of sticky anti-Semitic scuffles in Passaic. That Monday, the guys put me up against an opponent around my own age, and I had no trouble with the kid. The week wore on, and still I was coming out on top every evening, much to the chagrin of the older guys. After Thursday, when I went hard up the side of an older kid's head, the guys decided it was time for me to meet Frankenstein.

Frankenstein, aka Frank Stein, to me at least, really looked like Frankenstein from where I stood way down below him. He was big; but I was skinny and fast. We went at it, and moving around him, I got in a few good ones. Bottom line, he shook it off and took me to the cleaners, but not without him knowing he was in a fight. He went home with a bloody lip, for him unheard of, and I went home with a mouse under my eye and told Mom I got hit with a Spaldeen, a pink Spalding rubber ball used in New York City stickball games. I think she saw through the lie, and one day shortly after, asked if I would like to take guitar lessons. I told her, sure! But . . . while I loved my big old gut bucket guitar with the jewels and rusty strings that my dad found for me in a pawn shop, it didn't really play very well. She up and took me over to Sam Ash's music store on Utica Avenue. I picked out a black Harmony Archtop with a red sunburst, real cool, and Sam recommended a guitar teacher he thought would be good for me: Rector Bailey. Oh yeah . . . my life was about to change.

We phoned Mr. Bailey, arranged a date to meet, and he said to bring a loose-leaf notebook. I showed up, with Mom tagging along, to his house at 119 McDonough Street, two blocks above Fulton Street in the black neighborhood of Brooklyn. I walked into his parlor and was overwhelmed by all the instruments. A grand piano totally covered about a foot high with music and books, an awesome Gibson 350 electric guitar resting on its stand, two saxophones under the piano, a vibraphone like Lionel Hampton played, and an upright bass standing in the corner. It was scary cool.

He asked me if I was serious about playing the guitar, and I said, "Yes, sir." He warned me that I had to be prepared for my lesson every week and that meant practicing, and if I didn't, we'd have trouble. Without any fanfare, he sat me right down, checked out my guitar, and asked me to play something. Jeez, what could I play? I only knew stuff that I made up on the spot, so I improvised something. He asked me where I learned it, and I said, "I just made it up."

He looked at my mother and said, "I think we might get along really well."

He then took my notebook and wrote out diagrams of six chords for me to learn and named them. I was to memorize them and be ready to play each one as he called them out at my next lesson. "And I don't expect you to keep me waiting while your fingers are trying to figure them out."

I was sufficiently terrified, practiced like crazy, and was ready for him that next week. I breezed through it, and then he took my notebook and wrote out the chords in a certain pattern and put the book back in front of me. He sat down at the piano and said, "See those slashes under each chord? Just play those chords in rhythm, each time real smooth. I'll count off the tempo, and we'll start. You got it? Here we go . . ." And there we went. We played through his chart, and it was otherworldly. "How'd ya like that?" he asked.

"Did we just play a song?"

He laughed and said, "It's the classic ballad 'Blue Moon.'"

I lived and breathed guitar, practicing in the back of the trolley car on my way to school. I hung out in the record shop on Fulton Street around the corner from Rector's after my lesson, listening to jazz, gospel, calypso, and Latin music. "Hey, kid, you gonna buy something or what?" I usually left there with a used 10" vinyl single, 15 cents, one song on each side. I'd try to play along at home, memorizing the music, becoming a "member" of the King Cole Trio, Benny Goodman Sextet, playing behind Sister Rosetta Tharpe, a wonderful gospel singer and guitar player, putting into action everything Rector was passing to me. My ears were opening up to whole new worlds of music.

Sometimes on a Sunday afternoon, Dad would turn on the radio to WNYC's Symphony Hour, lie down on the sofa, and take a nap. Arturo Toscanini and the New York Philharmonic held forth, and I would take it all in. I would catch the subway up to the main library on Grand Army Plaza by Prospect Park and borrow records. One day, I borrowed Igor Stravinsky's *The Rite of Spring* (*Le Sacre du printemps*), after hearing it on the radio. It was wild, pure magic. I also borrowed the written score book with it and would follow the music even though I couldn't yet read a note. The library kept sending overdue notices, but I would ignore them for quite a while. Django Reinhardt and Charlie Christian became constant listens. There was that gypsy wildness in Django's playing that I wanted to emulate. One profound experience was the first time I heard the Indian sitarist, Ravi Shankar. *Where did HE come from? I found a photo of him with his sitar. How could he play like that on that huge bulky, THING?* These, the thoughts of a young teenager beginning to sprout his musical chops.

❁ ❁ ❁

One Sunday afternoon, I must have been around fifteen, Rector took me with him—jeez, how I must'a nagged him all the time—to a gig at a rally for The Workmen's Circle. I think it was some sort of a leftist socialist organization. It was being held in a hall across the street from The Cooper Union College of Science and Art in Greenwich Village. I carried Rector's big Gibson, and he took in his amp and set it up on stage, and then started mingling with the people who would be performing that afternoon. I followed him around, and suddenly he was talking to a huge black man. *Oh my god,* I realized it was Paul Robeson. I sidled up to Rector. Smiling, but very serious, he introduced me as his young protégé. Me? His protégé?

Mr. Robeson stuck out his hand and in his big, commanding voice said, "How nice to meet you. What instrument do you play?"

"Guitar, sir," I said, and then I don't know how I managed it, but I spit it out, "Mr. Robeson, I'll never forget when I was ten, my aunt took me to see you on Broadway in *Othello,* and you were wonderful. I'll remember it always. We sat way up in the balcony, but I could hear every word you said."

He laughed heartily, thanked me, and told me how the show had been a memorable moment for him as well.

Rector also spoke with the folk singer Josh White. Rector was going to back him up on guitar, as well as play piano for Mr. Robeson and whoever else was going to sing, without a rehearsal.

"How do you do that?" I asked him.

He said, "You have to listen to how the melody is moving through a song, and after a few years of listening that way, you pretty much know where the song's gonna go."

"Okay," I said, not really understanding, but I was learning.

The kid was growing up. My studies with Rector were totally consuming my life. Rector and his mother, Mamacita, were like a second family to me, and they actually were my first group experience. Mamacita, an accomplished upright bassist, would come in and sit on a high barstool playing time, Rector on piano, and me playing rhythm chords to the music he was giving me. Gradually, as I progressed, I was allowed to play the melody and take baby-step solos. *Was I cool or what?* Sometimes, after my lesson, Mamacita would make me a sandwich out back in the kitchen, and I had to fight off Monita, her pet spider monkey, to get it down.

Rector was also teaching me to read, saying I was ready because I was starting to get a real feel for my instrument, which he wanted me to have before introducing me to what he called technical stuff. He gave me exercises that he created in some basic keys, and soon put a sheet in front of me and said, "Take this home and play it for me next week." *C'mon,* I thought when I looked at it. *Really?* It was the first section of George Gershwin's "Rhapsody in Blue." He arranged it for guitar to include the chords and melody at the same time. Schoolwork be damned. This was my schoolwork, and yeah, I did it. Slowly, but I did it.

Yes, I was somewhat learning to read, but my ears were getting in the way of formal training, as reading music seemed mechanical to me, mathematical. Mathematics being a subject I never did pass in school, never had a passing grade. But math didn't get in the way of playing, just the reading of music.

I met a young, budding arranger, Garry Sherman, who was holding sessions at his house for guys to play his arrangements. He wrote one for "The Nearness of You" that included a guitar counterpoint part that was to be played against the melody. I could not even begin to read the chart, so I asked Garry to play it on the piano because there were a couple of places that I thought didn't sound right. He played the part, not realizing what I was up to. I listened to him play it, and then could immediately play it back by heart, without anyone knowing I hadn't read the music, just played it by ear.

After seventy years, I can still play Garry's "The Nearness of You" chart from memory, note for note. I never became a decent reader; my ears still get in the way. Nonetheless, I will forever be grateful for the gift that allowed me to hear magic in music, beyond reading the notes. It allowed my imagination to weave musical tapestries within Nina's music—wherever she chose to go.

MOMS MABLEY

BY THE TIME I was sixteen, I had been studying guitar with Rector Bailey for four years under his strict demands and expectations. With my folks' approval, he began taking me to his gigs on weekends. One weekend, he was appearing with his band, the Afro Cubans, at the Town Hill Supper Club, formerly the Bedford Rest, on Eastern Parkway and Bedford Avenue in Brooklyn near Ebbets Field, where the Brooklyn Dodgers played. It was a popular upscale club catering to the Black community. I always felt welcome and eager to play for the exceptionally appreciative crowds who seemed to support my playing and encouraged me as I came of age in those Brooklyn clubs. They were all great music venues, where I learned to hone my guitar chops: The Tip Top Club, The Arlington, The Coronet, Brooklyn Baby Grand, The Ebony Club, and The Kingston Lounge.

The guest performer appearing that weekend at Town Hill was Jackie "Moms" Mabley, a terrific stand-up comedienne and icon in the black entertainment world. Per usual, I was sitting in with Rector's band, playing songs he would choose for me, and then came the time for the main show. After an introduction, out came this older woman in a housecoat, apron, stockings half rolled down, bandana on her head, and sweeping the floor with a straw broom. Mom's signature entrance. She started across the floor, sweeping as she went, looked up, saw me, pointed, and yelled out, "WHA DAT??" The crowd roared. "IT WHITE!!"

The crowd roared even more. I looked at Rector for help, but he was laughing as well. "DAT A WHITE CHILE!!" Moms was now in front of me, I was up on the stage trying to disappear, and she said, "Chile, you so pale and skinny. You go home and tell you mama give you some chitlin's 'n greens and some chocolate milk, so you get some color in you." By then I'd melted into the floor, and the audience was rolling with laughter.

After a while, she let up on me, shaking her head with disbelief at what she had just come upon. She continued on with her hilarious act, and when she finished, we played her off and took a break. Rector led me backstage, and there was Moms talking to some people, and when she saw me she came right up and gave me an enormous hug, wanted to know my name, told me she was so sorry to take advantage of me and that it was all in fun. She hoped I was okay with it, said that I was a good sport, and would be out later to hear me play. We went back on for our set, and there she was sitting in the audience, applauding heartily.

A few years later, while playing with Nina Simone, I met her again at a festival in Atlanta. She remembered that night with the sixteen-year-old skinny white kid, gave me one of her big hugs and said, "Well, now, didn't you turn out real good," and, if Moms said so . . . .

FINANCIAL REALITY IN A MUSICIAN'S WORLD

I still had a long way to go before my magical and life-changing meeting with Nina Simone would take place.

AS I WAS COMING of age as a musician, I was branded a "klezmer" by my family, a word describing an itinerant musician in Eastern European Jewish ghettos. "He'll forever struggle to make a living playing weddings and bar mitzvahs to support his family. What nice Jewish girl would want that kind of life?" This is what would come at my mother when she sat around with her sisters and friends, once it was becoming apparent that I was going to be a musician. For sure, there were George Gershwin and Benny Goodman as examples of Jewish musical success, but it was like saying that a Goldstein could become president of the United States, and what were the chances of that? No, I would only bring "tzuris" (trouble and woe) to the family. As it turned out, "nice Jewish girls" never did take an interest in me, but then again, I never did take an interest in "nice Jewish girls."

When I was around seventeen, I had the idea that if I was going to seriously pursue a career as a professional musician, I should join the Musicians Union, New York AFM Local 802, as if those credentials would elevate me, give me some kind of status, someone to be taken seriously. I had to take an audition, and nervous as hell, since I still couldn't really read music and would have to go to my ears again, I walked into the audition room. The union reps told me to play a couple of chords, any chords. I did, and they said, "You're in."

"That's it?" I said.

They said, "You have a great career ahead of you, son."

Wow, wait'll I tell the folks.

My first union gig was at a Midtown Manhattan lounge, a gig that I picked up at the union floor, an afternoon meeting place for union musicians on Monday, Wednesday, and Friday at Roseland Ballroom. Musicians would congregate in cliques around the vast ballroom, looking for work, with someone sitting on the stage holding a microphone, making announcements about a gig or paging someone. The cliques were based on the types of music: pop, Latin, jazz, Broadway theatre, and club dates, which were usually weddings.

I picked up a gig that paid union minimum, which was eighteen dollars a night. Fifty-four bucks for the weekend, and man, was I cool or what? I was a working musician. It was just me and an older piano player whom I had never before played with. I set up my amp next to him over the bar and noticed his hands. He had two fingers on each hand, and otherwise had little nubs, instead of fingers. Amazingly, he could really play. Close your eyes, you'd never know. It was great playing with him, and at the end of the weekend, he wanted my phone number for future gigs. Looking back, I think no one wanted that gig at eighteen dollars a night. I'm sure the piano player was making more. On top of that, I had to pay the union rep who would show up for his dole. Ah, youth.

I have to tell you how I dressed. Remember, I was a teenager, this was the bebop era, and wow, was this skinny white kid ever bebop. Royal blue corduroy jacket, chartreuse dress shirt, black tie with maroon polka dots, maroon pegged pants, black wingtip shoes, and on my head, a tan fedora with a feather. I actually went to the gig dressed this way, and also showed up at jazz clubs dressed like this, lying about my age, trying to get in. "Well, here comes Mr. Cool." They sure knew me at the door. I'd be carrying my guitar, and they usually let me pass. Guess I added color to the scene. I was definitely not headed for weddings and bar mitzvahs.

I had come in contact with a small-time booking agent in the Brill Building on Broadway named Eddie Bart, who booked dates in the "Borscht Belt" in the Catskill Mountains. This was up where my parents' old farm was, and I thought maybe I could get a gig around there for the summer. I was going on eighteen and would soon have to register for the army draft. Oddly enough, he had a call from a well-known and somewhat outrageous club in Fallsburg, New York. The Wonderbar, looking for a bass player to fill out a quartet playing there. I had bought a bass, a big blonde mama, and was starting to get a handle on it with Rector Bailey's help. "Remember, Alio," he said, "the bass is the keeper of the time, so don't go and get fancy. Don't start thinking like a guitar player."

I told Eddie that I would take the gig. Seventy-five dollars a week with room and board. I rode up there on the bus and walked into The Wonderbar. There were two outrageous transvestite "barmaids," Toni and Bernie, holding forth, and a large showroom where well-known acts performed, such as Henny Youngman and Belle Barth, the foul-mouthed comedienne with her famous line, "If I embarrass you, tell your friends." It was afternoon, and the band was in the bar practicing. They were older guys. I introduced myself to them and asked the trumpet player if they played bop. "We play music, man," he answered, dismissing me. Ah, my education continued.

Meeting these musicians was a real awakening, interacting with established musicians who were not easily impressed with a kid entering their scene. I came to learn that jazz musicians, all musicians who can really play, are not easily impressed by a new kid on the block. You have to play your way in. Joe Shepley was the trumpet player. He would, years later, play lead in the trumpet section of my big band.

Even with the budding career, some years later, finances for gigs could be an unexpected challenge.

I had partnered up to play some gigs with my pianist and composer friend, Bob Dorough, later recognized for his fine musical contribution to the Schoolhouse Rock animated TV children's series, of which I was the guitarist. He was also the composer of the jazz classic "Comin' Home Baby" and the song "Blue Xmas" for Miles Davis.

Bob had worked with Ada Moore, the star of the Broadway musical *House of Flowers*. She was going to sing at her friend's new restaurant, which would be opening in St. Thomas in the Virgin Islands. The owner agreed to hire us as the house band. Arriving there with our families in tow, our wives and one toddler each, we moved into a beautiful house arranged by the club owner, situated on the locally famous Ninety-Nine Steps, halfway up a hillside overlooking the harbor in Charlotte Amalie. *Wow! What a nice scene,* I thought, especially since I wasn't currently working with Nina, who had recently given birth to her daughter. The club was on the waterfront, decorated with live flowers and plants, a small stage, and a fairly decent spinet piano. We met with Ada and began rehearsing her repertoire of songs.

The opening of the club was a huge success, tourists and locals mingling in what seemed to be a sedate tropical atmosphere, although I came to see that not all was well in this paradise. There were two diverse elements in St. Thomas: the wealthy expats and the poverty-stricken locals, who weren't seeing any rewards from the lucrative tourist trade. There were lots of rumblings going on from the St. Thomians.

Bob and I played an afternoon matinee when the cruise ships docked, in addition to our evening sets, and life was moving along pretty nicely, but I noticed after a month or so that business was falling off. It seemed as though the local crowds, the expats, weren't supporting the club scene. The owner was definitely in a financial bind. One day, he told us to hold down the fort while he flew back to Boston to secure more money from his investors. We did, continuing to play and drawing what little funds we could out of the nightly take. And so, we waited for his return. And waited and waited. Yup, he never came back, and the restaurant closed. Ada went back to the states and Bob and I created a gig at an outdoor bar, also on the waterfront, rolled the piano over, played for tips from the bar and busked the waterfront crowds. Actually, we didn't make out too badly. We made enough to feed the family and saved enough dough for our airline tickets home. Ah, paradise, or paradise lost?

DIXIELAND BLUES

IT WAS TWO A.M. when we hung a left on the old county road just west of Savannah, Georgia, heading out to Fort Stewart to play a Special Services gig. We stopped in Savannah and spent a few hours with some girls we had met at Birdland Jazz Club when we were up in New York on leave from Third Army Headquarters in Atlanta, Georgia, where we were stationed. Wynton Kelly had been sitting in on piano with Dizzy Gillespie's band, which he was a member of before he was drafted. Wynton was a wonderful piano player. Diz and Dinah Washington would always fight over him for his services. A few years later, he would be with the Miles Davis Quintet.

We had been socializing with the girls when suddenly there came a loud rapping on the door. It was the police, with guns drawn, asking about the army car out front. Wynton said it was ours, and we were on our way to Fort Stewart. They said, "Outside, all of you." They shoved us up against the car, spread-eagled, hands on the roof, and searched us and the vehicle, just hoping we stole it. Our papers were in order, but they shoved me, slapped me around, and said to get out to the base, and if they ever saw us in town again, "We will be the last thing you niggers ever see."

So! We were outta there real fast. Wynton was driving, and Duke Pearson, a fine trumpet player and arranger, was up front with him. I was in the back seat. We passed a closed gas station on the outskirts of town, took a left at a tee in the road out to the base, and then suddenly there were headlights in our rearview mirror. A pickup was coming up fast outta the gas station, and guys were shooting at us. Wynton floored the pedal on the Chevy that we had checked out from our motor pool. We had no weapons on us to fire back at them, and desperate, I picked up a wooden clothes hanger, stuck it out the window, and screamed like a banshee "BAM BAM BAM" . . . *Sure! That'll work.* The chase was on, Wynton snaking down the road with Duke folded up under the dashboard and me in back yelling and holding my "gun" out the window. We were outrunning them, me "shooting" all the way. They finally turned around as we approached a little strip mall near the base, and Wynton yelled back to me, "Nice shootin', Al."

I'm talking 1954. We were deep in Jim Crow's Georgia. Wynton and Duke are black, the girls are white. *How did those rednecks know where we had been?* Sure, easy enough to figure out. The cops must have called the "boys" and told them where we were headed. And what about those poor girls? They were locals. *How were they ever going to live in that town after this?* Y'know what I'm sayin'?

I hadn't realized the culture shock that awaited me in Atlanta when Wynton got me transferred into his Special Services outfit after I had completed basic training at Fort Dix, New Jersey. Wynton was older than me and had been drafted a year earlier, this being during the Korean War. We had been sitting in with the band at the Kingston Lounge in Brooklyn, while he was home on furlough, and he told me if I pushed up my draft, I wasn't expecting to be drafted for another year or two, he could arrange to get me into his outfit's traveling road show as the band's guitarist. Wynton was sure he could make this happen, as he was a favorite of General Bolling, the commanding general at Third Army Headquarters, which oversaw all the army bases in the southern United States.

My flight touched down in Atlanta, and I collected my duffle bag and walked into the terminal. I needed a restroom, and looking around, I saw the two men's room signs. White. Colored. Oh boy, I said to myself, what do I do now? I sure as hell don't want to go into that redneck bathroom, so I just up and headed for the colored one, knowing I would feel much more comfortable being among black folks. In I went and was promptly stopped by the attendant, who yelled at me, "Boy, get the hell outta here, can't you read the signs?"

I was in uniform and said, "I just landed here, in from New York, and I sure don't want to mix with them rednecks."

Now the other men in there started laughing, and the attendant said, "Son, that's all well and good, welcome to Georgia," and he kicked me out. Such was my entree into Southern society.

When I arrived at Fort McPherson, the band was away playing a show at a base in Alabama. I was given a bunk in the dorm-like barracks of an ivy-covered building that you might find on a New England college campus. The building also housed a country western band that played the same bases as Wynton's show. They were rehearsing, and I was introduced to the guys led by Faron Young, the country singing star who had been drafted along with a couple of his band members.

Faron was a real gentleman, welcomed me, was glad to see me on board with Wynton's group, and invited me to sit in on their rehearsal. "I hope Wynton is back by tomorrow because I need him on piano for a show I'm playing this weekend at the Fox Theater downtown." *What? A black piano player in a white country band in the South? Or anywhere? In 1954?* I must have had a weird look on my face, because Faron laughed and said, "Jazz music aside, Wynton's about the finest country piano player I ever came across, and if he's in Faron Young's band, ain't no one gonna say a thing." *Okay,* I thought, and unpacked my guitar, hooked up my amp, and joined in, never having heard of most of his songs before. One thing about good country music is that it's all about the story, the ballads sweet or sad, the up-tunes rousing. Simple, like the blues. I really enjoyed the session, playing some solos and backing up Faron on a couple of ballads. After we were done, Faron said, "You're lyin' if you tell me you never played these songs before."

I said, "No, but I used to like to play some folk and mountain stuff when I was a kid, never really knew what I was doing."

"Well, you sure know what you're doing now. How would you like to join us for my show next weekend?"

"What? Well, sure, if you're sure, I'd like that a lot. I've never heard Wynton play country. Should be a blast."

As it turned out, Faron had a couple of big hit songs on the country charts, "If You Ain't Lovin'," and "Goin' Steady." What is odd is that he was also singing pop songs with the Third Army Dance Band, having replaced none other than Eddie Fisher. And, wow, that dance band was monster good. I met some great musicians, who remained good friends after my army days.

Pianist Jerry Rabinowitz, a fantastic world-class musician who also played bassoon; bass player Al Quagliatta, both he and Jerry from New York. Also, soulful tenor sax man Al "Black Dog" Wright, from Biloxi, Mississippi. I learned he was disinherited from his wealthy white pharmacy-chain family for preferring to socialize in the Black community rather than "his own kind."

Wynton got back from his road trip, and I met the guys in the group. Among them, as I mentioned earlier, Atlanta's Duke Pearson, a fine trumpet player, who would later switch to piano, and become an acclaimed jazz arranger for big bands, and George Joyner, who later, as Jamil Nasser, was the bassist with the legendary pianist Ahmad Jamal.

Duke lived at home, off the base, and one weekend, the first time I went home with him, he led the way through the gate to his house, and his little daughter, she was three or four, came running out to greet him. He picked her up in his arms and lovingly said, "How's daddy's sweetest little nigga?" and she just giggled. *Huh? Did I hear that right?* Later, I asked Duke about it, how he was using what was to me the worst thing one could say to a child, and he said that no matter, as his daughter grew up, if that word was thrown at her in a racist way, she would remember hearing it as a loving thing from her daddy. Later on in my life, I heard the "N" word used between each other by my black friends, and indeed Nina Simone used to call me nigga as well. It felt good, hearing that, when she came at me in her endearing way. But look out, you didn't want to hear that when she was angry.

I did play Faron Young's show, with Wynton Kelly on piano. Faron gave him a big solo on a hot honky-tonk song, introduced him, with the crowd giving him a rousing applause. There you go. Music transcending Jim Crow . . . at least for that moment.

I have to say, my time in the army turned out to be an important step in my musical life, as well as my personal development. I went in as a kid and came out a young man.

DON'T LAUGH:
A HILARIOUS AND AWKWARD MOMENT

MY THREE FRIENDS and I were invited to the Orthodox Jewish wedding of Jerry Rabinowitz. It was to take place at the bride's parents' apartment in the Bronx, just across from an elevated subway train near Yankee Stadium. Inviting us to this wedding was Jerry's first mistake. Jerry was a great jazz piano player, a very feisty and terrier-like little guy. His feistiness was far exceeded only by his petite, miniature terrier-like betrothed . . . Alice.

Jerry's second mistake was asking us four friends from the army to be the pole holders of the chuppah, a canopy over the bride and groom during their ceremony, symbolizing the house of the groom and the new domain of the bride. This is an ancient and solemn ritual legalizing their marriage under Orthodox Jewish law.

Now we get to us, four "Musketeers," bordering on rascals, one might say. Rudy Guarnaccia, superb drummer, nearing seven feet tall, tough Sicilian New Yorker. Al Quagliatta, fine bass player, 250-pound tough, and also a Sicilian New Yorker. Barry Newman, later to be known for his portrayal of Kowalski in the movie *Vanishing Point*, and for his title role in the 1970s television series *Petrocelli*, and me, the skinny white kid.

After we were instructed about the pole responsibilities of holding up the corners of the chuppah, we decided that some spiritual support was needed and, unobserved, left the crowded living room of chattering guests for the quietude of the bathroom, whereupon Rudy came forth with a big fat doobie. Barry opened the window, and we lit up on some extra fine Panama Red, any noise being made blowing smoke out was drowned by the roar of the elevated trains going by. Nicely fortified, one by one, we rejoined the guests and took up our pole positions with the ceremony about to begin. These poles were broomsticks with a nail sticking out from the top, the grommets of the chuppah loosely set on them.

The ceremony began, the bride and groom safely under the chuppah, with the rabbi reading the marriage liturgy. This is not a quick service, no "do you take" and "I do's" or "I now pronounce you." No such luck. About twenty minutes in, with trains occasionally drowning out whatever was being said, we were about halfway through, and suddenly, Big Rudy had some itch on his rather expansive nose that he had to attend to. While holding the pole in one hand, he started rubbing his nose. The pole leaned over, and the corner slipped off the nail, flapping down on Alice. I leaned over to get Rudy's corner, my corner slipped off, and then both Alice and Jerry were lost under the canopy. Quagliatta started laughing, good smoke can do that, and it set off Rudy, Barry, and me as well. This set off Alice screaming, "What the hell? Goddam it, Jerry, you invited these bastards, do something!" Real sophisticated Orthodox Hebraic language. Jerry began screaming slurs and curses on us and our families. We were laughing outrageously, spurred on by the Panama Red, while the rabbi and guests were trying to get the canopy off the bride and groom. Order was finally restored, the chuppah back in place with others now holding the poles, and we, four Musketeers, quietly disappearing. A blessed start to wedded bliss.

One day recently, the phone rang, and out of the blue, after almost sixty years, it was Jerry Rabinowitz, sounding jovial and so happy to make contact. He had seen reviews of the Nina Simone documentary that premiered at the Sundance Film Festival and wanted to reach out. He told me that he had cancer and was going to pass in six months.

He sounded great, and we were chatting about old times for a while, when he suddenly yelled out, "Alice, come here, Al Schackman is on the phone and you can say hello."

She yelled back, "Hell no, tell him to get lost, and hang up the damn phone."

Well, after thinking back on that whole time, I have to say I hold a warm place in my heart for Jerry, a huge respect for his masterful musicianship, and hope he achieved the highest levels possible in his life . . . with all due respect to Alice.

NINA SIMONE: PRELUDE

I WAS DISCHARGED from army service in October of 1955, and I eagerly looked to jump back into the New York music scene. I took the first gig that came along. It was on bass at Club 59 on East Fifty-Ninth Street, around the corner from the Bloomingdale's department store. Fortunately, I owned a big upright bass and had been playing bass a lot in the army, so I thought I could handle it. The gig was with a trio headed by legendary pianist Ram Ramirez, the composer of the classic ballad "Lover Man." The drummer was the great New York session player, Rudy Guarnaccia. How lucky I was to find this steady six nights a week gig. It was a privilege playing with Ram, but he left shortly after I joined the trio, and we replaced him with Jerry Rabinowitz, our feisty piano-playing friend. A guy used to come in and sit by the bandstand, usually with a drink in his hand. He said he was a comedian, and down on his luck, and that he also played drums. Rudy took pity on him and would let him sit in. He wasn't too bad and kept the beat. A couple of years later, I saw him sitting behind his desk on the *Tonight Show*. Yup, Johnny Carson. *Ya never know.*

One night, a patron came in, really listened to the band, came back a few nights later and bought the band a round of drinks. His name was John Francis, and he told us he had a restaurant, the Canal House, on the Delaware River in

New Hope, Pennsylvania. The town was an artist colony and home of the Bucks County Playhouse, one of the country's foremost repertory theatres. He said he would love to have us as his house trio through the summer and early fall. Our pay would include accommodations and dinner. We jumped at the offer, and in June, we began the gig. It was just an hour and a half drive from New York City, where I retained a loft in Greenwich Village.

We returned every summer for the next couple of years, and one night, in the summer of 1958, a group of people were at the restaurant for dinner. After hearing me play guitar, they approached me about possibly sitting in with a friend of theirs, Nina Simone, who they said was a virtuoso musician playing solo piano at the Bucks County Playhouse Inn nearby. Always curious about any so-called "virtuoso" musician, I said, "Why not?" They came back the next evening, having gotten her okay and arranged for us to play together that Sunday night when I was off. I showed up while she was on a break and, not seeing any familiar faces around, plugged in my amp, tuned up, and waited for her. After a few minutes, she appeared on stage and, without even saying hello or acknowledging my presence, began playing a Bach piece, "Good King Wenceslaus." I have perfect pitch, an innate ability to identify a note, so I knew what key she was playing in and joined her, developing counterpoint and fugue, challenging each other, with Nina still not even acknowledging me being there. We were totally improvising, totally jazz, totally classical, totally mind-blowing, and at the height of it, while this incredible interaction was going on, she softly began singing the ballad, "Little Girl Blue." She then looked up at me with a coy, little smile on her face. *Whoa, Nellie, we were in uncharted waters.* We played out the set with some blues and another ballad, "I Loves You Porgy."

Afterward, her friends introduced us. She extended her hand and said very formally, "How nice to meet you. Would you be interested in visiting for tea next Saturday afternoon?" *HUH?* She was done for the night and was about to drive back to Philadelphia, where she lived. I said I would be delighted, and was given her address. As she was going through the door, she turned and said, "Oh yes, and would you please bring your guitar."

On Saturday, I drove out to her house in West Philly. She lived in a sunny upper-floor apartment that I reached by climbing open wooden stairs that were on the outside of the house, similar to the tenement houses on Chicago's Southside. Nina greeted me at the door, very cheery, told me to make myself comfortable, that tea would be ready in a few minutes, and showed me where to plug in my amp. Well, she did serve tea and cookies, told me how wonderful it was to meet a musical kindred spirit, and that she had never played with another instrumentalist until the other night with me.

She asked where I had gotten my formal training. I said that if she meant like Juilliard or Curtis Institute in Philly, I didn't have any. She was dumbfounded and said that was impossible because I was inventing fugues and classical counterpoint with her. I said, "Uh-huh, tell you about it later. Let's play." And did we ever.

I wish I had a recording of that afternoon. Two straight

hours of incredible music, including Duke Ellington, blues, romantic ballads, and, of all things, folk songs. Nina was very formal, swinging but shy, weaving classical forms throughout her solos. I could tell she was new at interacting with another musician.

In a flash, it was five o'clock, and I had to get back to New Hope for my gig that evening. Nina invited me to play with her again at the Playhouse Inn on Sunday, and said she was bringing a conga drummer with her, whom she had just met. He turned out to be Al "Tootie" Heath, the brother of Percy Heath, bassist with the Modern Jazz Quartet. We played that night, and once again it was incredibly innovative music, with Tootie nicely complementing the evening. Thus began a magical ride of forty-six years with the incredible woman dubbed the "High Priestess of Soul," who would become an international star and civil rights icon.

After that summer, I was back in New York, hosting jam sessions in my eighty dollars a month Greenwich Village loft, playing gigs in clubs around town, and doing R&B studio sessions for Atlantic and Columbia Records with the Isley Brothers, Bennie King, Solomon Burke, and The Drifters. I had just teamed up with pianist and singer-songwriter Bob Dorough. Bob booked us some gigs on the West Coast, and one day, just before we were set to leave, I had a call from Nina. She was coming to New York, had some club dates, and was signed to record an album for Bethlehem Records, and would I be available. *Why did that ball have to bounce just at the time that the Dorough ball hit my backcourt?* Bob and I had a great thing started, and I had to pass on Nina's invitation. She wound up doing the album with Jimmy Bond on bass and Tootie Heath on drums. Nina's recording of "Little Girl Blue" from that album became a legendary classic. I'm still upset about missing out on that session. Sadly, she sold away her recording rights for 3,000 dollars, while the album made a bundle.

When I returned from the West Coast, I contacted Nina, and she hoped I would join her for gigs. She wanted a trio behind her, and what a trio we became! Ron Carter on bass, Ben Riley on drums, and Al Schackman, me, on guitar. We played at Max Gordon's Village Vanguard in New York, Peps and The Showboat, two of the best jazz rooms in Philly, and at The Blue Note in Chicago, Baker's Keyboard Lounge in Detroit, and George Wein's Storyville in Boston. Our trio would play a set and then bring Nina on. Playing with Ron and Ben was a joy. It was seamless between the three of us, and add Nina to the mix? *Alvin,* I would say to myself, *you gonna get arrested.*

Ben left the group to go with Thelonious Monk, and Ron went with Miles Davis. Me? I went with Nina and Baba Olatunji to Africa, but more about that later. Bassist Chris White and drummer Bobby Hamilton replaced Ron and Ben, and this group became the foundation of Nina's large body of work during that era.

EXCERPT FROM NINA SIMONE'S AUTOBIOGRAPHY

I Put a Spell on You

" Although jazz musicians are used to improvising, they need to be familiar with how another musician plays before they can really get something going; they have to listen and get their minds on the same track, or they get a lot of hesitations and false starts. But when I started in on *Little Girl Blue*, Al was right there with me from the moment, as if we had been playing together all our lives. It was more than that even: it was as if we were one instrument split in two, I, the piano, Al, the guitar. I had never felt so much freedom in playing, knowing that someone knew where I was going, and I knew where he was going. It was like telepathy—we couldn't lose each other. And Al had perfect pitch, too, so I never had to tell him what key to play."

MY ADVENTUROUS MUSICAL EDUCATION

NINA HAD ASKED me that day at her house in Philly about my formal musical training. I really had no short explanation as my education encompassed a diverse progression of study, none of which was formal in Nina's understanding of formal.

There were piano lessons for a short while, when I was six, that ended abruptly after the teacher angrily slapped my hand when I played my own variation on the lesson, and, while showing me how she wanted me to play it, I closed the piano lid down on her hands. She screamed. My mother ran in, was told I was unteachable, and after paying her and seeing her out, Mom came back in. I told her what happened, and she just shook her head and laughed.

Another piano teacher was found. She was mainly interested in bringing her friends to watch the little boy call out the notes with his eyes closed after she played them. Big deal, I had perfect pitch, as did Nina Simone, I learned later.

I have to say that at the heart of my musical training were years of instruction with Rector Bailey in Brooklyn, learning how to listen, really listen. Respecting the space between notes, the silence being as important as the sound. He told me to allow the guitar to breathe and let it speak, not blither like mind chatter. Meanwhile, I was not being steeped in reading and would later find myself lacking in this area of music.

I was twenty-two and enrolled in composition and theory at Columbia University under the GI Bill after getting out of the army. I lasted only a year, frustrated because I still could hardly read music. I took up classical guitar in New York with Alexander Bellow, a Russian friend of Andre Segovia. He really helped me create a personal fingerstyle, playing chords similar to the way a harpist might play them. The method was really nice behind a horn or vocalist doing a ballad.

New York City, "the Apple," had people arriving every day chasing their dream of "making it," but me? I was already there, guitar in hand, right at that moment in the music scene when the guitar was screamin' off every R&B, rock, and pop recording.

We were heading into the 60s. Atlantic, Columbia, RCA, Capital, as well as the independent recording studios, were going nonstop, and me, this skinny white kid, found myself right in the thick of it, getting calls for recording sessions.

The first recording sessions that I was involved in were, oddly enough, with an Armenian band led by a fantastic musician, Chick Ganimian, whom I had recently met. He played the Oud, a Middle Eastern bowl-shaped lute, and asked me to join his band, playing gigs with him on rhythm guitar. Middle Eastern music and belly dancing were the current rage in the city, and we played in a revue at the Round Table nightclub on Manhattan's East Side, as well as other clubs and private events. That's how I learned to play in more exotic time signatures. We "Westerners" are used to singing and dancing in 2/4 (polkas), 3/4 (waltz), and 4/4 (pop, R&B, jazz, and blues) time. Middle Eastern rhythms also include 5/4-, 7/8-, and 9/8-time signatures. These rhythms became easier for me to understand as I watched the flow of folks dancing when we played at Armenian weddings.

Chick was a close friend of Ahmet and Nesuhi Ertegun, the founders of Atlantic Records. Chick's band was signed to record an album in order to test out the studio's new equipment. Multitrack recording was just then becoming a reality, sixteen separate tracks on two-inch-wide recording tape. Their studio was located in Manhattan, just below Columbus Circle, in a small office building. The control room was so cramped that there was only room for the recording console. The sixteen-track machine stood out in the hallway. Tom Dowd was the engineer, and he, through the years, became a legendary recording engineer. The album, *Come With Me To The Casbah,* included a few American standards such as "My Funny Valentine" and "Somewhere Over the Rainbow," as well as traditional Middle Eastern music. Those sessions helped launch me into the New York recording scene.

I became a first-call session guitarist for Atlantic Records, as well as Columbia, under John Hammond, who was celebrated for discovering Bob Dylan, Bruce Springsteen, and Aretha Franklin, among dozens of other artists. John phoned one day to tell me about a new find of his, a Nigerian drummer and singer, Michael Babatunde Olatunji and his Drums of Passion. He wanted to merge New York jazz musicians with Olatunji's group of musicians and singers and asked if I would be available for the sessions. *For SURE, Mr. Hammond.*

Meeting Baba would be an inspiration for me. I would be introduced, close up, to a direct source of African music. It was an incredible experience. I became close with Baba, I introduced him to Nina Simone, and he taught us some of his songs, which Nina recorded and performed. He invited us to an international music festival in Lagos, Nigeria.

I still have to smile at the Yoruba name Baba bestowed upon me. *Shanki Ogidan, he whose roar can make even the leopard in the forest tremble with fear.* I asked him what it was he saw in me to give me that name, and he said, "*Al, I would not want to be the target of your roar. Do you not feel it there in you?*"

I did learn to recognize Shanki Ogidan, especially when music was not being performed properly or without feeling by those around me. I continued to play with *Olatunji and The Drums of Passion*, off and on, for well over fifty years, learning the beauty of African music and the Yoruba culture.

Garry Sherman continued his outstanding contribution to my musical knowledge and development. He had become an award-winning recording producer and arranger, a film composer writing the score for *Midnight Cowboy* and *The Heartbreak Kid*, and on top of all his musical accomplishments, a doctor of sports podiatry. Of anyone who took me under their wing, so to speak, it was Garry who made the effort to teach me to read music.

I learned recently that the block I had in reading music was actually a condition I might have, recognized by the inability to learn math, and there is a mathematical relationship to reading the rhythms of a musical chart. *I mean, five times failing the remedial math course in high school? Hmm.* The condition is called dyscalculia. Interesting because it is believed that a person with dyscalculia might otherwise excel in music, art, or design.

Garry was encouraging me to learn to read music charts,

putting together a nine-piece band of some great musicians, who he was going to have perform at Birdland, the top jazz club in New York City. And what a group it was! Phil Woods and George Young on alto sax, Frank Foster on tenor, Pepper Adams on baritone, Joe Shepley and Jerry Gonzales on trumpet, Milt Hinton (Uncle Miltie) on bass, Bernard (Pretty) Purdy on drums, and me on guitar. Taking the place of the piano, I was to read charts in order to play that role on guitar, and sometimes I was to read the charts and play as part of the horn section, as well as soloing. I had a "photographic memory" when hearing music. I could retain the music after hearing it only once, which was very counterproductive to trying to improve my reading skills. But Garry wouldn't let me avoid reading the darned charts. So weird, because I can write music, score music for movies, but reading music? Ha! Today I do read, with thanks to Garry, although I'm not great at it.

We did play that Birdland gig; it was very well received. I even stood up to play my solos, which drew laughter from the guys in the band. In a large band, the guitar player traditionally never stands, but so what, I thought, I earned it. After all, I was now a chart reader. Thank you, Garry, with my deepest appreciation of our friendship.

NINA SIMONE AT THE APOLLO THEATER

PERFORMING AT THE Apollo Theater is an achievement that, for a Black artist, might surpass even Carnegie Hall. For this skinny white kid, appearing at the Apollo was an exceptional honor, especially as the guitarist with Nina Simone.

"Hey, you must take the A train if you wanna get to Harlem," says Duke Ellington and Billy Strayhorn in their classic song, "Take the 'A' Train."

Getting off the A train at the 125th Street subway station, you are a two-minute walk from the Apollo Theater, the citadel and showcase of Black theatrical entertainment in America since 1914. Its historic role throughout the years in the emergence of swing, jazz, bebop, blues, R&B, gospel, and soul music is unparalleled.

Amateur night at the Apollo Theater is a raucous and critical make-or-break evening for an aspiring young performer. Singer, dancer, comedian, taking the Apollo stage in front of a highly critical, knowledgeable, and highly vocal audience can be a daunting, sometimes devastating, career-ending experience. The crowd will boo you right off the stage in a second if they don't like what you're about, and in the old days, might also bring overly ripe vegetation to throw at the poor soul to back up their critique.

On November 21st, 1934, seventeen-year-old Ella Fitzgerald placed her name in the hat, hoping to be picked to perform, and, to her surprise and trepidation, hers was one of the names chosen. She was going to do a dance routine, but a group of dancers that were on just before her were much better, she thought, so she instead decided to sing. She went out, sang "The Object of My Affections," brought the house down, and won the evening.

Dionne Warwick told this story. When Dionne was sixteen, she participated with her sister and cousin as The Gospelaires, in an amateur night before the Apollo's Wednesday evening show. She was very nervous waiting backstage. Nina Simone, who would be performing later that night, walked up to her and said, "Listen here, girl, you go out there and make that stage so hot that whoever comes out after you will have to walk on tip toes."

February 10th through 17th, 1961, we were headlining at the Apollo for one week and had just finished our afternoon set. I was backstage, wanting to hear the James Moody Band and sit in on a set with Sonny Stitt's Band, who were also on the bill. Sonny was a giant among musicians; his alto sax sound was so close to Bird's, (Charlie Parker), that the two of them would challenge each other as to who was copying whom. After a rehab stint at Federal Narcotics Hospital in Lexington, Kentucky, in 1949, Sonny abandoned the alto and switched to tenor saxophone, transferring his wonderful sound to that horn. I was up in the musician's dressing room talking with Sonny and some band members when his young drummer came in, looked at me, and yelled, "Hey! What kind a shit is this? What's whitey doin' in our dressing room?"

"*WHERE*," I cried. "*Who let him in?*" as the guys cracked up laughing

Sonny spoke up and said, "Billy, meet Al, he's Nina Simone's guitar player. Be cool now, this nigga can play. He's gonna sit in with us on our next set."

That shut him down, but he didn't really let it go.

I did sit in on Sonny's set, and during one of my solos, the drummer played some explosive rhythm breaks during my pauses, which I picked up on, and thinking he was trying to intimidate me, I repeated some of his phrasings into my solo. Like having a conversation. After the set, he came up to me, apologized for acting out upstairs, and said, "Sorry for jumpin' on ya, man, you're alright."

I was honored when, later, Sonny asked me to play with his organ trio for a gig in Cherry Hill, New Jersey. It would happen during the time that Nina would be taking off for a few weeks after performing a concert at the University of North Carolina at Chapel Hill. Perfect timing for Sonny's gig.

I was standing around when Tadd Dameron came up to me. Tadd, an iconic arranger and pianist, whose writing influence can be heard in the work of many of today's big band arrangers, was playing piano and arranging for James Moody's orchestra. He said that he had been listening to me play with Nina and thought highly of what I contributed to her classical style. "Al," he said, "with the addition of your counterpoint to Simone, the sound is unique. You don't hear that in jazz today other than Dave Brubeck and his alto player. Well done."

Indeed, Dave and Paul Desmond, his alto sax player, did that together beautifully. Their composition "Blue Rondo *à* la Turk," as an example. I was really impressed that Tadd Dameron had taken the time to listen to our set. He ignored Nina's shenanigans when she first went on stage. Those shenanigans were a real Nina Simone "rumble."

Here's the way it went down.

Even being new to the major stages, Nina's reputation was already preceding her. She's difficult, promoters and club owners would say. She can be rude to the audience. She might not show up for the performance, or once there, not go on stage until she's paid first.

Being aware of Nina's temperament, the powers that be at the Apollo Theater were not fools. They wanted to make sure Nina would get to the stage. Sure, they figured, no problem. We'll pay her up front in cash as she demanded, but we'll put it in an envelope and sit it on the piano. She'll have to come out on stage to collect it and, hopefully, we'll get on with the show from there.

SHOWTIME. I stood just offstage, waiting for Nina to come from her dressing room. She and I would usually stand on one side of the stage and the rest of the band on the other side, ready to come out after the introduction. Nina came from her room and said, "Hold on, Al, before I play one note, I'm going out there and get my money," and with that, in her elegant gown, she walked out to rousing applause from a full house. Ignoring them, she sat down at the piano, picked up the envelope, opened it, and started counting out the money. Now, this was a big wad of cash because much of it was in small bills that had been collected from the box office. As she counted the money, she put it in piles across the piano lid to keep count.

When she was done and satisfied that it was the correct amount, she picked up the wads and put them all back in the envelope. She then turned to the audience, and in her eloquent voice said, "Good evening."

Suddenly, Nina grabbed the envelope of cash from the piano, stood up, and as if in slow motion with the back of her legs beginning to tip the heavy concert bench over, she started to sit back down but sat on the edge of the bench, which, with Nina's backside in tow, was then in the process of falling on its side. This resulted in Nina slowly falling back with the bench, and her sitting with her backside on the floor and her legs up over the side of the bench. The audience, stunned as this scene was unfolding before them, was then in uproarious laughter. Someone in the audience yelled out, "*WE LOVE YOU, NINA,*" Nina yells back, "*NO, YOU DON'T!*"

"YES, WE DO!"

"NO, YOU DON'T!"

By then, Honi Coles, the stage manager, along with a couple of his crew, ran out and picked up Nina. She was still holding on to the envelope of cash and yelling at the audience, who was chanting, "WE LOVE NINA, WE LOVE NINA." He got her to her dressing room, and we played a short set while Nina put herself back together. After a couple of songs, I looked offstage and saw Nina coming toward us with a glass of champagne in her hand. She just walked on while the crowd cheered, sat down at the piano as if nothing had happened, and jumped into a rousing intro to "Just in Time," a great rhythm tune that we all enjoyed playing. From that point on, the evening was a huge success with Nina firmly in control, gracious, having a good time with her fans, and in one final moment, thanked them, saying with a playful tone in her voice, "You were a wonderful audience tonight. I really fell for you."

CABARET ID CARDS AND THE NEW YORK CITY POLICE DEPARTMENT

NOT KNOWN to many people, years ago in New York City, there was a requirement that anyone working in an establishment that served alcohol had to obtain a cabaret or police ID card in order to be employed. If denied this card, mainly due to an arrest, even if not having been convicted, the person would not be allowed to work in said establishment. Any such place that broke this so-called "law" (it was never passed by the New York State Legislature), would have its liquor license suspended or revoked. This jurisdiction encompassed all restaurants, hotels, nightclubs, and cafés within New York City boundaries. Any bartender, hat-check girl, dishwasher, waiter, musician, anyone who ran afoul of the long arm of the NYPD was denied employment.

After a summer of playing with my trio in New Hope, Pennsylvania, I was back in New York in a new trio playing at The Den, a nightclub in the Hotel Duane on Madison Avenue and Thirty-Seventh Street, featuring avant-garde entertainers such as Lenny Bruce, Mike Nichols and Elaine May, singers David Allen and Johnny Hartman and comedians George Carlin, Lord Buckley, and Milt Kamen. I myself did hold a police card, obtained a couple of years earlier, just after being released from the army, and didn't feel compelled to inform the NYPD of my marijuana arrest that previous summer in Pennsylvania, hoping that it wouldn't raise its ugly head back in New York. I didn't realize that by playing at The Den I was going to be in the thick of the fight, led by attorney Maxwell T. Cohen, that was gathering momentum to dismantle the NYC police card system.

Max was representing, free of charge, David Allen, trombonist J. J. Johnson, pianists Bud Powell and Bill Rubenstein, and most notably, popular comedian Lord Buckley, in their attempt to acquire or reinstate a police card after being denied their applications by the Police Card Division of the NYPD. David Allen, with no police card and with the knowledge of Eddie Leipzig, The Den's manager, was appearing there, backed by my trio. Eddie was under obligation by the Police Card Division, as were all establishments in NYC that held liquor licenses, to list the names of all employees and their IDs. He refused, and his liquor license was suspended for three days, shutting us down, typical of the harassment going on throughout the NYPD's jurisdiction.

The Den became a rallying point, and Max became the "commanding general" in the war. One night at The Den, I had just arrived for the gig, Eddie came up to me and said, "Al, if you or the boys are carrying any drugs, pot or whatever, get rid of it immediately because I just got word that we could be raided by the police." In fact, Lenny Bruce, who was known to be a heroin addict, was appearing that week, and Eddie had immediately, upon having been tipped off, gone into the dressing room and "cleaned up." A good thing he did, because the police indeed came in and searched the place.

Many people were denied a livelihood because of this underhanded and illegal police activity. On November 12, 1960, Lord Buckley, unable to find employment, died in poverty.

For those who aren't familiar with him, he was a hilarious and insightful comedian who, for over many years, entertained millions, performed for troops in war zones, casualties in hospitals, and was a champion of civil rights and social justice. His death made all the New York newspapers, and Ed Sullivan paid tribute to him on his national TV show.

A Citizens' Emergency Committee was quickly organized, and a meeting was held at George Plimpton's apartment on the Upper East Side of Manhattan. The list of people attending was a who's who of distinguished writers, composers, musicians, actors, and other public figures; dozens of people who knew Lord Buckley. Among them were many friends and acquaintances: playwright Lorraine Hansberry, actor Theodore Bikel, Elaine Lorillard, one of the founders of the Newport Jazz Festival, and musicians Dizzy Gillespie, Stan Getz, and Quincy Jones. I talked with Nina about going, and she was really up for it. We arrived at a packed apartment, and the place was buzzing with an excitement of purpose. This was the organized response that the NYC police department needed to have stuck in their face. It was still going to be a battle, but now the commissioner was going to find an army at his doorstep. Lord Buckley's family had requested a hearing to posthumously obtain a cabaret card for him, and Max agreed to appear at the hearing.

The tide did turn. It was found that there was never a legal statute that initiated cabaret card legislation, and after more battles with the Police Card Division, letters were sent to then-Governor Nelson Rockefeller by the Citizens' Emergency Committee and Maxwell T. Cohen in order to make him aware of the situation. It was clear that the cabaret card system was dying, and after ambiguous changes to the system and, after the police commissioner was dismissed by then-Mayor Robert Wagner, the system was abandoned. Musicians and other cabaret workers regained their constitutional right to gain employment, and an ugly stain on the City of New York was erased. Above and beyond everyone who participated in the struggle, Max stands at the forefront.

SWEET MOMENTS WITH NINA

I LIVED ON RIVERSIDE DRIVE and West 158th Street, below the George Washington Bridge. Nina was living on Central Park West and 101st Street in a top-floor apartment overlooking the park. It was 1960, and we were being booked pretty well, working at the Village Gate and Village Vanguard as well as clubs in Philadelphia, Boston, D.C., Detroit, and Chicago. Nina knew I was into cars and asked me if I would find her a car to buy, something nice and exotic.

West 158th Street from Riverside Drive is a steep hill connecting down onto the Westside Highway entrance and Riverside Park on the Hudson River. Along the street was a foreign car repair shop where I had my car garaged and serviced. One day, while I was at the garage, I saw a beauty of a 1958 Mercedes 220 SE convertible sitting there. The mechanic told me it was a special edition; the owner had to sell it and was asking $5,000. With a gunmetal grey finish, red top, red leather seats, red carpeting, and burled wood paneling, it was exquisite.

The mechanic, Karl, said, "Lift the trunk." and WOW! sitting on the carpeting was a three-piece set of custom-fitted red leather luggage.

"Karl, don't move this vehicle. I'll be back soon." I ran up to my apartment and phoned Nina. "Nina, I found your car.

$5,000 takes it. Get over here now and bring some money to hold it."

"I'll be right there, shugga."

Twenty minutes later, I was waiting outside my house, and a cab pulled up and she jumped out. She was wearing a sweater, jeans, sneakers, a bandana on her head, and yelled, "Show me my car." We ran halfway down the hill and into the garage. She saw the car and said, "Oh yeah, that's MINE! Where's the keys? Let's go for a drive."

Karl got the keys and handed them to Nina.

"Hell, I don't know how to drive this thing, Al, you drive."

She gave me the keys, we got in, and off we went onto the Westside Highway and headed north, under the George Washington Bridge and onto the Henry Hudson Parkway, the car tooling along smooth as can be.

"Faster, Al. Let's see what this thing can do."

"Nina," I said, "too many curves on this road. Besides, this isn't a sports car, just an elegant drive, just right for you."

"Awright, awright," she said, pouting. "But just wait 'till I learn to drive it."

"Oh, Lord," I said, "please watch over this gal when she gets to it."

Nina bought the car, and she really did have some fun with it, even though she had it in the garage a lot because she never got the electric shifting right.

One afternoon, Nina phoned and said, "I'll pick you up in ten minutes. We're driving down to the Village to meet up with Richie at the Village Gate." Richie Havens was a good friend, outrageous, outspoken, always ready to stand up and be counted when it came to the serious and dangerous civil rights business going down at the time.

She was out front in ten, and we got onto the West Side Highway, the top down, sunny day, Nina with a scarf around her neck, blowing in the wind. She turned to me and yelled out, "I'm Grace Kelly in that movie." Oh yeah, suddenly she turned into Grace Kelly, talking like her and all. That was Nina—she could transport herself into whatever she wanted to be and wherever she wanted to go, beyond race or color, like a chameleon, into any personality or character. That was the magic one experienced in her music.

We met Richie at the Village Gate's sidewalk café and had some lunch with the rumble of Bleecker Street traffic rolling by a few feet away. Of course, the talk got around to civil rights, revolution, the role of music in the resistance, maybe doing an album together, and although it never came to bear, in 1971 they each recorded George Harrison's "Here Comes the Sun," both beautiful renditions, with Nina's on the Billboard charts for four weeks, but Richie's for fourteen weeks, reaching number sixteen.

Whenever Richie was in the audience, Nina would have him come up on stage for support, and he would clap rhythm or echo her, just fun stuff. She did that with James Baldwin as well. Jimmie would come up on stage, just sit on a bar stool, and "be there" for her. A momentary relief from feeling alone.

There were times when having someone come up on stage didn't work so well for her, though. At the Heritage Music Festival in New Orleans, Baba Olatunji and his Drums of

Passion were on the bill. He was a close friend, by then, having invited us to the AMSAC International Cultural Festival in Lagos, Nigeria. Nina invited him up on stage during our set. She introduced him, and he came up to such a huge ovation that Nina got angry, started yelling at him, and chased him off the stage. "You can listen to him on his own time," she told the audience, "not mine."

That's our Nina, gotta love her.

A RAINY NIGHT WITH NINA IN NORTH CAROLINA

IN 1962, NINA was invited to perform at the University of North Carolina. Unusual, as it was still the segregated South, but Nina was now a famous North Carolina girl, and the college was excited to have her. *How "nice" of them.*

We decided to fly down early on the day of the concert and fly back that night, in order to avoid having to deal with lodging. The concert was highlighted by Nina admonishing the packed house of students to demand for integration at the school. Did the administration think that Nina would just quietly come and go? That was their hope, but we learned that our flight was canceled due to weather, which changed everything. That meant the only way back to New York was on the Champion, a streamliner train running from Miami to Boston and coming through Chapel Hill at two a.m. It was ten p.m., and we were looking at a four-hour wait. We were driven down to the station with all our gear: Nina's suitcase, Bobby Hamilton's drum kit, Chris White's upright bass, my guitar and amp. The station was a dinky one-room building that had its heyday back in the thirties, with a ticket man nodding off in a room behind the counter.

The accommodations were typical of Southern "hospitality" of those times, separate black seating, water fountains, and restrooms. There was just one other person waiting for the train, an elderly white woman looking none too happy when we startled her awake by our sudden appearance. For those who have never been in the land of Ol' Jim Crow, you can read about that shit all you want, but you will never get it in your gut the way you will when you're standing in it. And that's just this skinny white kid talking. Imagine going into a train station in Nazi Germany and seeing a bunch of people in a corner wearing a yellow star sewn onto their clothes, standing under a sign that read "JUDEN." *Does that get it for you any better?* Of course not, but same thing, same difference. Same old, same old racism, alive and well in the USA.

We were hungry and, leaving Bobby to stay back and mind our gear, Nina, Chris, and I decided to try to find a black diner that might still be open on this cold and wet, miserable night. We walked through some deserted streets, definitely not the white part of town, and lucked out and found a place that was closed but had some lights on. We knocked and a young girl came to the door and said, "We's closed. I'm just cleanin' up." Nina went into her "attitude," took out a bunch of bills, and "ordered" her to make us some sandwiches. Chris jumped in and told her how we were waiting down at the station for the late train to New York and would be grateful if she would help us out. She had no idea who Nina Simone was, but she very nicely went back into the kitchen. She came back out after a while with a big bag of food and said, "That oughta' hold ya for the ride." We left her a nice bunch of money, and as we were leaving, she called out in true Southern style, "Y'all take care now."

As we made our way back, we saw a flashing red glow coming from the train station. With a collective "uh oh," we picked up the pace, and sure enough, standing in front of the station was a police cruiser with its lights going. In we went. Standing in front of us were two officers who had Bobby in handcuffs, and that old lady who had been sitting across the way in the white section was hysterical.

Bobby was shaking like a leaf and started to tell us what was going on, "Nina, I was fast asleep and . . ."

A cop said, "Shut up, we'll do the talking." They proceeded to tell us, "While this lady was asleep, this colored boy stole her handbag, and he won't tell us where he put it. So we're takin' him in to get the truth outta him."

That's all Nina had to hear to get her engine revved. "Now listen here, you two, I'm Nina Fucking Simone. This man works for me, and he makes more money in one night than the two of you make in a month. So you better get those handcuffs offa him right now or I'm gonna put you in some trouble you won't forget."

The cops looked at each other. Apparently, they never ever had heard a black man, and especially not an "uppity" black woman, talk back that way. "Girl, you're about to get your own black ass arrested," he said. On that, Chris and I jumped into our Brooklyn attitude. Chris said, "The two of you going to try and lock us all up? That'll be interesting."

The cops, now riled, were ready to get into it.

Suddenly Nina yelled, "I've had enough of this shit, where's my phone book?" and pulled it out of her purse. "I'm going to call Terry. That's Governor Sanford to you. He's a good friend of mine."

Indeed, he was, and a big fan of the homegrown North Carolina girl.

"I have his home telephone number right here, and I'm sure it'll ring right by his bed. Of course, it's after one in the morning, and he'll be real happy to hear about your behavior. Where's the phone?"

Well, now the two cops were scared. They started backpedaling. "But, Ma'am, we're just here to protect you if there's any trouble. See? We're takin' the cuffs offa him right now, and we'll get to the bottom of the lady's missing purse."

Nina said, "Shit, I'll get to the bottom of it myself." Nina looked around, and suddenly bolted into the White Ladies' Room.

"Lady, you can't go into the . . ." yelled one of the cops.

She came out a second later with the woman's handbag, walked up to her and said, "Found this by the toilet. Yours?"

The woman just stuttered, "Well, I . . ."

Nina looked down at her. "You belong in the toilet with the handbag, lady. Here!" and handed her the bag.

The cops said, "Sorry for the misunderstanding. We'll be outta here if there's nothin' more we can do for ya," and off they went.

The South was changing, albeit there was still heavy resistance to what was coming. Governor Terry Sanford, an early champion of civil rights, called out the State Police to protect civil rights demonstrators and protected the Freedom Riders when their bus came through North Carolina. The times they were a changing, as the song goes, but on that one rainy miserable night . . . the times hadn't changed fast enough for us.

The Champion rolled in promptly at two a.m. We boarded, sat down, opened that bag of food, and man, we found fried chicken, biscuits, and a tub of potato salad, which we passed around. That young kid even put in plastic forks and napkins. We ate, looked at each other, and just shook our heads.

Bobby looked over at Nina and said, "Nina, you sure know how to do it when the shit goes down."

She laughed and said, "I take care of my boys, shugga. Them peckerwoods didn't stand a chance."

Nina was right on, and as Bobby said, "She was always front and center when the shit went down."

We were a band of Brothers and one fine Sister.

A STORMY NIGHT FLIGHT WITH NINA

ANDREW STROUD, Nina's husband and now our manager, had us scheduled to fly to New York on an early flight the day after a performance in Chicago to perform that night at Carnegie Hall. Nina was already complaining about being "worked like a dog," and this added fuel to her fire. The weather was real nasty with heavy rain and wind. After being delayed, we got word that our flight was canceled and so that evening's concert was in jeopardy. We were booked out on a 707 jet, which couldn't fly in that weather. Andy phoned around for a possible charter and found a DC3 aircraft that could fly under the cloud ceiling. Andy booked it, and with luck, we would land at LaGuardia Airport around a half an hour before going onstage. With luck. I mean, it was pouring. We all looked at each other with trepidation. So many artists have gone down in air tragedies, and I was thinking of the headlines, *Nina Simone and Band," etc., etc. . . . bet they wouldn't even spell my name right. Schackman, I said to myself, get that crap outta your head, you don't need that kinda energy right now.*

Our band, at that time, included Gene Perla on bass, Weldon Irvine on organ, and Don Alias on drums. After take-off, they were each taking a turn visiting the restroom, trying to deal with the heavy turbulence that the plane was going through. The old DC3 sloshed through the rain and eventually bumped us down into LaGuardia with fifteen minutes to curtain time.

Vehicles were waiting. We loaded our gear, and with Nina cussing all the way into town, we made it to Carnegie Hall. We jumped out, unloaded, threw off our coats, ran straight to the stage, and set up our instruments, with stagehands placing microphones while we tuned up. Nina came out, still wearing her coat, took a bow to a big round of applause, sat down at the piano, and went into a huge dialogue about the flight. How she was being "worked like a dog," and the audience should appreciate how we almost got killed trying to get here flying on some old piece of junk. In the middle of this tirade, she stopped cold, threw off her coat and said, "Aw shit, let's play," and went into the song "Just in Time," playing wild arpeggios, striking her heavy Rachmaninoff chords, singing away while we laid down some smooth swinging rhythm behind her. We all shook off the flight, got past the queasy stomachs, really got into the music, and the evening eventually turned out to be a blast. A real Nina Simone "happening."

SOARING WITH NINA SIMONE

I SHARED MANY wonderful moments with Nina Simone through the years. Here's a sweet one.

In 1985, Nina was living in Nijmegen, a small college town in the Netherlands on the Waal River, in order to be close to our Dutch friend, Gerrit Debruin. He had found her a small condo next door to the Belvoir Hotel, where I stayed to rehearse for concerts with her.

One June day, Nina said, "We're going for a ride in the country."

"Anyplace in particular?" I asked.

"You'll see when we get there."

Ohh-kayy . . . another Nina surprise. I brought her car around, and she met me out front dressed in yellow Bermuda shorts, a light-blue T-shirt, and a New York Yankees baseball cap atop her head. With me behind the wheel, off we went, Nina navigating. The Dutch countryside at that time of year was spectacular; fields and fields of flowers on a palette ablaze with color across the landscape. We drove for over an hour, at ease in our familiar and mostly nonverbal way with each other, when suddenly Nina pointed to a dirt road ahead on the right and said, "Take it." We followed that road, and after a while, I spotted a few low buildings a ways in the distance. As we got closer, I could make out Quonset hangars with some sailplanes parked around them.

"Uh, Nina, what are you getting me into?"

She giggled. "You'll see."

In the years that I had been with Nina, I had learned to expect the unexpected, and here I was again, presented with a new ripple. We were going soaring, and obviously she had done this before, as I found out when we drove up to the airfield and parked. A couple of guys strode up to us and said, "Miss Simone, how good to see you again. We're all set to fly." Hmm, evidently she had phoned ahead. I was introduced, and we were led out to the sailplanes. Now, don't misunderstand me, I do love an adventure, but I had come to realize early on in our relationship that I should always be keeping an eye out for trouble, as Nina had an uncanny gift for finding it. But amazingly, this looked like it might possibly turn into fun. So after taking a deep breath, I said to myself again, *Ohh-kayy, and off we went.*

The sailplane team had a unique system for launching their aircraft. At one end of the dirt runway, they had an auto engine hooked up to a huge spool of steel cable. The planes were towed down to the opposite end of the runway, and the cable, with a hook on it, was brought down and attached to the nose of the plane. These were two-seaters; the pilot got in and Nina jumped in behind him. The engine downfield was revved up, and the spool began winding faster and faster with the sailplane rolling down the runway and soon airborne. Up and up it went, the pilot released the hook, and they soared into the sky to catch the thermals.

Then it was my turn in the other sailplane. In I jumped, and we repeated the same process. Up we went, unhooked and climbed into the blue sky. We were around two thousand feet, quietly, majestically soaring on the wind, lazily circling on the thermals, when suddenly the pilot pointed out the left side, and there across from us was Nina's plane with her laughing and waving at me. The feeling up there was timeless. We soared around with the pilot showing me the controls and letting me take over for a short go. Eventually, we made our way back to the field and landed. Nina ran up to me, threw me into a big hug, and yelled at the top of her lungs, "Al, you SEE? THIS is being alive, REALLY alive."

The guys invited us for a beer. They were a great bunch. It turned out that they were a sailplane club, all licensed to fly and train, one fellow a schoolteacher, another an accountant, but ALL of them huge Nina Simone fans.

We drove back to Nijmegen totally at peace with the world. How rare for Nina. We went down to the riverboat restaurant on the Waal near her home for a nice dinner. We raised our wine glasses . . . Nina sparkled and yelled, "L'Chayim, to LIFE."

MEETING BRUCE LANGHORNE AT THE AMSAC FESTIVAL IN NIGERIA

BRUCE LANGHORNE, Bob Dylan's first guitarist, my dear, dear friend and cohort . . . *Where to begin?* I first started hearing about him, Bro Bru Bru, around 1960 at The Bitter End on Bleecker Street in Greenwich Village, a major center in the East Coast folk scene. I was playing at clubs in the Village and with Nina Simone at the Village Gate, just across the street from The Bitter End. I kept a small guitar amp there to use when I sat in with the folk crowd. On breaks, I would haul my guitar over, hook up, and sit in with various artists and groups. As a kid, I started out playing folk and western songs on my old gut bucket guitar and enjoyed that music.

Folk music was opening up to new contemporary sounds, and I believe I was the first electric guitar on the scene. I think they liked having Nina Simone's guitarist, a jazz guy, bring an amplified sound to their music. If the purists didn't appreciate it, they didn't say so to my face. Theo Bikel, a folk artist who had starred on Broadway as Tevye in *Fiddler on the Roof*, hosted a Sunday afternoon radio show for WNYC. Tongue in cheek, he would introduce me as "Sparks." *I sure was their novelty.*

I would sit in with artists like Fred Neal, Tim Hardin, Judy Collins, Bob Gibson of Gibson and Camp, Jim (Roger) McGuinn, and Ian and Sylvia from Canada, along with David Bromberg and Sandy Bull, a couple of really fine acoustic guitarists. Bob Dylan would walk around the tables during intermissions with his harmonica and guitar, entertaining the audience. He was among the new wave of folk artists coming up.

People kept telling me about this guitar player, who had only two fingers and three stumps on his picking hand, and that no one could do the things he could do with a guitar. They were talking about Bruce Langhorne. "Al, you and Bruce have to get together. You'll blow each other's minds," I was told. I kept hearing about him, but he was never around when I was. I heard he backed up Odetta and the gospel singer Brother John Sellers, so he was on the road a lot. *Well,* I thought, *someday it's bound to happen.*

In December of 1961, Nina Simone and I were invited by Nigerian drummer and singer Michael Baba Olatunji to participate in an international music and cultural festival in Lagos, Nigeria organized by the American Society of African Culture. Baba had just recently gained acclaim for his *Drums of Passion* album on Columbia Records, which I had played on. Also attending were other leading American artists, musicians, writers, and educators from the Black community, who would be interacting and performing with African artists, writers, and educators. Among the group were Lionel Hampton and his band, Odetta accompanied by Bruce Langhorne and Bill Lee, Brock Peters, opera singer Martha Flowers, gospel singer Brother John Sellers, and the great jazz pianist Randy Weston with his quartet featuring tenor saxophonist Booker Ervin. Also invited were dancer Geoffrey Holder, poet Langston

Hughes, and Dr. Horace Mann Bond, dean of the School of Education at Atlanta University, and the father of civil rights activist Julian Bond.

Our Alitalia flight landed in Lagos late at night, and when the cabin's door was opened, the overwhelming, intoxicating scent from the jungle filled the cabin, and the sound of an army of drums and singing filled my ears. A welcoming party of dozens of drummers and dancers was there to greet us, along with government dignitaries. This was not a modern airport; the landing field was carved out of the jungle, and huge fires were burning to light up the night. The stairs were lowered, and our entourage descended, everyone on board feeling that they were returning to their ancestral home as African brothers and sisters. As the only non-black person in the group, I keenly observed the emotional wave running through everyone. They were referred to in the welcoming speech as "our American cousins," not brothers and sisters. Not quite what some of my friends and colleagues had imagined. Still, it was a joyous reception, and after the formalities, we were taken to the Federal Palace Hotel, a sumptuous estate, which had been the site of the recent signing of the Nigerian Declaration of Independence.

Later that night, I was hanging out in my room with a few musicians, when there came a rap on my door. I opened it and standing there, waving his stumpy hand, was a guy smiling at me.

"Al," he said.

Of course, I knew him immediately. "Bruce," I said, and we plowed into a huge embrace, as might lifelong brothers. "I know you," I said.

"I know you," he said.

We had been told about each other for so long, and finally now we meet, not in Greenwich Village, New York, but one very late night in Lagos, Nigeria. Thus began our brotherhood of music, crazy adventures, and deep respect that lasted fifty-eight years until Bro Bru Bru's passing on April 14, 2017.

The afternoon after arriving, we were invited to a banquet hosted by President Nnamdi Azikiwe, the first president of the newly Independent Republic of Nigeria. He was considered to be the father of Nigerian Nationalism. We were ushered into a grand hall with tall louvered doors facing out to tropical gardens and a long table set for at least fifty guests. President Azikiwe was seated at its head, and I had been seated near the opposite end by a huge open window. Hanging from the ceiling were beautiful silk fans undulating back and forth, creating a gentle breeze. I noticed a rope on pulleys slowly activating the fans, and curious as to the mechanism involved, followed the rope running the length of the hall across the ceiling, down the end wall near me to the large open window and there, sitting on the outer ledge of the window was a young boy maybe ten years old, barefoot and with the rope tied around his foot, moving the fans back and forth. I smiled at him, and he grinned back at me and gave me a little wave. Never mind horsepower, I was looking at a one-boy-powered engine. *How wonderful, the president of Nigeria is hosting an international gathering, and the air conditioning is operated by a little barefoot boy with a rope tied to his foot. If only the world could be this simple.*

The banquet ended in the early evening, and I was relaxing back at the hotel's patio with Bruce, Randy Weston, and his tenor man, Booker Ervin. We decided to explore the grounds and walked out a good distance beyond the gardens, and after a while, we found ourselves at the edge of the forest. It was very dark, and we were completely surrounded by mist except for a clear circle directly overhead, filled with the brightest stars I had ever seen. We just stood there, enraptured by the sounds of life emanating from the forest, feeling as though we were in some exotic temple.

Suddenly, Booker whispered in his inimitable vernacular, "My brothers, I thinks we ain'ts alone." Sure enough, we looked around and there in the mist, someone stood watching us. He came closer, and we saw that he was in uniform. He was dressed in a khaki jacket, epaulets on his shoulders, short pants with high socks and boots, and on his head a fez with a tassel and gold badge. He was also carrying a rifle. It was like he had just stepped out of a Lawrence of Arabia story. Speechless, we all looked at each other for a few moments.

Then he said in English with a deep lilting accent, "Gentlemen, good evening."

We replied, "Good evening," while nervously regarding his rifle.

"What brings you to the edge of the forest in the late of night?" he asked.

I told him that we were here for the music festival, guests at the Federal Palace, and were just out walking, exploring the land.

To our dismay, Booker piped up, "Hey, my man, do you know where we can score some grass?"

The soldier looked confused. "You know, some weed?"

Booker said. The soldier, still confused. "Reefer, a joint, a doobie, ya know what I'm sayin'?" No response.

Then Bruce chimed in, "Say, my brother, where can we find some ganja?"

"Oh, ganja," he laughed. "You want ganja. Wait here. I will go to my house. It is nearby."

"Well," Randy said, "that was a little too straightforward, Booker. It could have caused us some trouble."

Booker replied, "Nothin' like get'n to the point."

We were relieved when the guard came back a little while later and presented us with a huge doobie rolled in thin airline paper. We thanked him. He told us he had to continue on with his guard duties, and then said very seriously, "Do not stay here very long, as you don't want to meet the leopard who hunts in this forest."

We just looked at each other. "Leopards?" I said, as Booker lit up the smoke, but after passing it around, we were no longer worried about the leopard. Surely we were safe, in our temple, floating away up there under the stars.

The next day, everyone was busy preparing for the opening of the festival that night. Rehearsals, interviews, meetings with the organizers, going over the program. The concert would run over two nights at the King George V Stadium.

Nina and I were really excited about being in Africa for the first time. We were rehearsing some of her songs with bassist Abdul-Malik and drummer Clarence Stroman when she suddenly looked up at me and said, "Al, how do you feel being the only white person on the scene? Don't you feel strange?"

I said that I hadn't thought about it, as it often happens.

"But," I said, "if you want me to put it into words, I feel lucky and honored to be accepted into what I consider to be my Black family. You know I came up in the Black community, and I'm more at home in it, not only musically, but culturally and socially, than in any other scene."

"I know that," she said, "but can you understand what it means for me to look around and know that I am in a nation where me and my people are in the majority? Here I'm not a nigga in the White man's world. But," she said laughingly, "now you're HERE. Now you're a nigga in the Black man's world." We both broke up laughing, and she said, "I love you, shugga."

I said, "Thank you. I love you, too. At least you call me nigga, nigga."

Abdul and Clarence looked at us, wondering what just happened, where in hell had we gone? "Uh, guys," Abdul said, "you just left us." Such was the relationship with me and Nina. Most people, white folks, don't ever get to hear the "N" word used with love and endearment.

The concerts were terrific, with a mix of African and American artists trading performances through the two evenings. The stadium was overflowing with people. Babatunde Olatunji and Clarence Stroman played a drum incantation to introduce the evening, and then Langston Hughes and Bobby Benson spoke and introduced the performers. It was surprising how well Lionel Hampton was received. The crowd roared, yelling "Lio-nel Hamp-tun, Lio-nel Hamp-tun," over and over. This jazz vibraphone legend was hugely popular and appreciated here in Nigeria. I wondered how that came about.

Olatunji sat in on our set, and he and Nina both sang his

composition, "Zungo," which he had recently taught to Nina and that she later performed on her Colpix Records recording, *Nina Simone Live at the Village Gate.* Among her program of standards at the festival, she sang "Love Me or Leave Me" and "Little Girl Blue," where we used our classical inventions. Nina also chose a gospel, "Children Go Where I Send You," which really got the audience going.

Bruce accompanied Odetta and Brother John Sellers. I also accompanied Brock Peters, who had played Crown in the movie version of *Porgy and Bess* that also starred Sidney Poitier as Porgy, Sammy Davis Jr. as Sportin' Life, and Dorothy Dandridge as Bess. I have to mention that the movie was heavily criticized for the characters being stereotyped as "Uncle Tom," and check this out, Dorothy Dandridge, one of America's foremost Black vocal artists, had her songs overdubbed by Adele Addison, an African American opera singer. You never got to hear Dorothy's wonderful voice, thanks to the Hollywood movie machinery that held sway during that era.

Both concerts played to a capacity audience. Every performer was wildly appreciated, and the festival was an event of the magnitude never before seen in Nigeria.

The morning after the last concert, Bruce and I were in the hotel dining room having breakfast when we were told that a tour of the old Yoruba quarter had been arranged, and we were to meet out front shortly. I ran to my room, grabbed my camera, and phoned Nina's room.

"WHAT?" a sleepy Nina replied.

"A tour of the old traditional tribal quarter has been arranged, and we're to meet shortly out front," I said.

"Al, I'm sleeping, and I've seen enough natives last night at the concert. See ya later." And she hung up.

"Whatever," I mumbled to myself, and off I went.

We all met downstairs, maybe fifteen of the group, and piled into two Volkswagen buses. We drove through the downtown area, past gleaming high-rise office buildings, people of all colors on the street. I asked Joseph, our Yoruba driver and guide, about that, and he said that Lagos had a large German and Swedish presence living there. He said that the native quarter was home to the Yoruba and Hausa people, who followed traditional tribal customs, and for the most part didn't integrate with modern Lagos. We would find the atmosphere somewhat like the Caribbean. We arrived at the drop-off point to the quarter, and nearby on vast lawns were women washing clothes in huge soapstone tubs, laying them out on the lush green lawns to dry. A kaleidoscope of colors in front of our eyes. Different shades of indigo and purple. These, we were told, were the dyes common to Nigeria. Joseph took us to the entrance, a dirt street that was filled with shops, where we could find traditional food and things to buy. "Maybe meet back in an hour. The buses will wait here," he said.

Bruce and I took off to explore on our own, and we walked into the village, browsing shops that were really just tent awnings with living quarters in the back. A butcher shop where the meat was hanging from hooks out in the open. Grains, vegetables, and fruit in abundance. We bought some food, had a delicious, spiced beef wrap in a bread that was like a Greek gyro, and washed it down with a beer-like ginger drink. We came upon a shop that sold tribal masks and talking drums. The drum's sound when you squeezed the straps created the inflections of the Yoruba language, hence the "talking" drum. Bruce bought a real nice sounding drum, and I bought a large, fierce-looking forest deity mask.

Amazingly, when we stopped at the shops, if someone saw Bruce's damaged hand, they would grab it and give a wail, say something to his hand, and want to take us into their hut for a tea. At least that was what they indicated, as no one spoke English. What we learned later was that the people looked on Bruce's hand as an omen, a sacrifice, that he was touched by God and was to be honored and esteemed. Welcoming Bruce into their abode would act as a good omen for them in the eyes of God. Bruce cordially let them hold his hand, laughing and exchanging good vibes, as only he could do.

Filled with delicious food and happy with our acquisitions, us two new-old brothers made it back to the buses, where most of the group had already gathered. After we waited around for a while, Joseph said that the big man was still not back, the big man being six-foot-nine Randy Weston. He was worried that Randy might be lost, and noticed Bruce's drum. "May I borrow your drum, mister?" he said. Bruce handed over the drum and mallet, whereupon the guide put the drum's strap over his shoulder, the drum in the crook of his arm, and started beating on it, squeezing with the inside of his arm, voicing the notes of the Yoruba language. As we learned from Randy later, at least a quarter mile away, a little old man walked up to Randy, pulled on his jacket and said, "Your people want you to go back now." When Randy showed up a little while later, Joseph returned the drum to Bruce, and we were all amazed.

Bruce asked, "Joseph, what did you say with the drum?"

He replied, "I said to tell the long American to come home now."

Bruce and I were totally in sync with each other and looking for adventure. We had fulfilled our obligations and were ready to get out on our own, and asked Joseph if he had any suggestions. He told us about the University of Nigeria in Ibadan, that the city was rich in culture and history and worth a visit. We could go by bus and it would take about two to three hours, depending on traffic, or we could rent a small boat with a motor, travel around the Lagos Lagoon, and visit some native villages. That sounded more like our kind of adventure, and we asked Joseph if he would make the arrangements. Unfortunately, we hadn't paid attention to our visas and learned that they wouldn't permit us to extend our stay. We were stuck with our group and would be leaving in two days. We decided to hit on some nightlife, and Joseph said he would take us to where the best band was playing.

"Al, you bring your guitar and amp, and I'm sure Victor, he plays the trumpet, will want you to play with the band. Victor Olaiya and the Cool Cats has the hottest record out, *Adelebo Tonwoku, (Single Lady Looking for a Husband)*." He laughed and said, "It's about a woman. If she wiggles her bottom and finds a husband, she should forgo her education. Last year, Victor played at our independence party that Princess Margaret attended. They are a great band for dancing."

"Okay," we said, "lead us to the music."

I told Nina about going to hear the band, and she said, "I'm ready to dance and meet a man. Count me in, but don't ask me to play. I'm just gonna dance and have me some fun."

The club was outdoors, with colored lights, low bamboo walls, tables around a large dance floor, and a big bandstand at the far end. The band had not started yet, and Joseph said he was going to find Victor and introduce us. He came back a few minutes later with Victor, who immediately said, "You are playing with us tonight," and grabbed my amp. It wasn't a question. I followed Victor to the backstage, and met the band, great guys, excited to have me play. They set my amp onstage, and we tuned up. He had a good-sized horn section, bass, two guitars, drums, the works. Victor said, "Joseph told me about you, so I know you will hear our music." And did I ever. I knew the songs, even though I had never heard them before. I played rhythm, and Victor gave me solos. I felt the guitar players digging my moves. A magical night that ended too soon. I didn't want to go back to New York. I wanted to join the band.

One of the guitar players came up to me and asked if I would sell him my amp. It was impossible to find one like that in Lagos. He said he could pay me in British West African pounds that would equal my dollars. I really felt happy for him to have it, and settled on two hundred dollars. It was less than what I paid, but I could buy a new one and wouldn't have to lug it back to the States with me.

The band pulled up chairs at our table, met Bruce, and were awed by him. One of the guys handed him a guitar, insisted he play something for us, and Bruce awed them with some soulful riffs. We sat around, drinking beer and talking music, with one guy talking a mile a minute, going on about music being on the front lines for fighting against social and political injustice. He was the guitar player who also sang and wrote songs. His name was Fela, who, of course, in the years to come, would gain international fame as a musician and political firebrand. We were having a blast but, suddenly concerned, I looked around for Nina and saw her across the way holding forth with a bunch of admirers around her. She grinned and waved. The girl was cool.

On our last day, we just relaxed at the pool. Nina was happy. She said that even though she didn't catch a man, she danced and flirted with many, got a little tipsy, and thanked me for putting her to bed.

"No problem, sweetheart," I said, "you were out like a light before you hit the pillow."

"Yeah, how strange," she said. "It's been a long while since I had a real good time, I can't even remember. Thank you, shugga."

The next day, we boarded the plane, back to our corner of civilization. Everyone filled with their own bag of thoughts and memories to take home with them, and mine filled with Bro Bru Bru and me finally coming together, with a world of adventures ahead of us.

PETER, PAUL AND MARY

ONCE WE WERE BACK in New York from Africa, Bruce Langhorne and I were hanging out and playing at jam sessions. One night at The Bitter End, Bruce and I played a blues set by ourselves. Damn, if only it had been recorded, it was terrific. Afterward, we ran into Mary Travers and Albert Grossman, who was Peter, Paul and Mary's manager. They were a new group and were going to be recording their first album for Warner Brothers, and Grossman asked me if I would be interested in coaching Mary with her vocals. He was worried that her habit of singing sharp was going to stand out in the recording. He knew of my work with Nina Simone, had heard me do backup for folk singer and guitarist Jo Mapes, and thought that I might be able to help Mary. It turned out that Bruce was going to play on their session, and so I agreed to see if I could help her. Mary wrote down her phone number while Bruce gave me a look that said, "We need to talk."

Later that night, he and I went over to the Four Brothers Diner on Sixth Avenue for some food, took a booth, and Bruce said, "Al, good luck with Mary. A couple of things you should know going in. She loves to have a good time, and when she sings, she just throws her long blonde mane around and belts out the song. Forget about her listening to the other guys in the group or caring anything about what she might sound like. She thinks she's at a Hootenanny. If you can get her to at least listen, it would be a miracle. What I'm saying is you might have to keep her focused, and yourself, too, lookin' like she looks," he said with a big laugh.

I got together with Mary at a little apartment she kept on MacDougal Street in the heart of the Village, and we worked on her songs up until the session dates, with her finally getting that I took it seriously, especially when I cussed her out about her attitude. She was a five-foot ten-inch, blonde, "stop traffic" beautiful, and maybe thought that it bought her a free pass. At times, it was difficult to focus, but I had a strong sense that she was on an express train going somewhere big, and I managed to stay on point, no easy matter with a strong attraction to each other. I think I did help her, especially with listening carefully to the music around her in the right way. Of course, I still had to ward off the mischievous looks that Bruce would give me.

I attended the recording session, standing in the hallway and looking through the porthole window of the heavily insulated door. Bruce was sitting in the studio opposite the door, saw me looking in and started making faces at me, putting his finger in his mouth like he was gagging. I was worried that he was trying to tell me that Mary's voice was out of tune, but he said later Mary sounded really good, and that he was just having fun because he was bored with the music, and I was a handy diversion. That's my Brucey Boy.

The album was a smash hit and launched Peter, Paul and Mary's fabulous career. I must say that Mary brought a freshness to the folk scene, bringing some glamour and flair into that old traditional world. I was right; Mary WAS on that express train, and her beautiful self surely DID go somewhere big.

KIM NOVAK:
OR JUDY BARTON . . . OR MADELINE ELSTER

The two characters brilliantly portrayed
by Kim in the film Vertigo.

IN 1963, WHILE LIVING in Big Sur, California, I was at a small gathering at Hollywood film set designer Eduardo Tirella's cabin. Present among the group were friends Jim Coburn, James Garner, and director Jack Haley, Jr. I had brought my guitar and was jamming with Peter Ind, a fabulous British double bassist who, after living in New York, had gone to Big Sur wanting to meet author Henry Miller. Putting down new roots, he convinced me to drop my studio gigs, my New York life, and move out there to explore that beautiful, truly magical land.

Coburn was a collector of rare Asian percussion instruments used in Buddhist temple ceremonies, gongs, meditation bells and bowls worthy of a museum collection, and would bring newly found pieces with him when visiting. He passed them around for us to play, or as he put it, have a "Buddhic" jam.

At some point, in walked a woman wearing jeans and a big sweater, looking quite rustic, homespun. Just a hometown gal. Except for her voice. One can never mistake that signature voice. It was Kim Novak. Eduardo ran to her, and after a big hug, brought her over to meet everyone. He had told her about me being Nina Simone's guitarist, said that Kim was interested in taking guitar lessons, and might I be interested in helping her find a guitar? I saw that Kim was familiar with Eduardo's effusive flamboyance, and we left it unsaid that she and I would pick it up by ourselves later.

During the evening, I noticed Kim lying down in Eduardo's loft, looking out at us from her perch. Hmm, I climbed up the ladder and lay down beside her with our heads poked out over the edge, observing the scene below, just comfortable side by side. After a while, I said, "Is Eduardo just gabbing, or are you really interested in learning to play?"

She then looked at me and said, "I'm serious about wanting to try. I can't promise how good a student I'd be, but I write, and I think some of my poems could be turned into songs. Most of my days are spent painting, but I can make time to practice."

"Well," I said, "I have a classical guitar that you can borrow to start with, and then we can find you a guitar if you want to continue."

"Let's get together tomorrow afternoon at my house. I live in Carmel Highlands, where are you?"

I said that I had recently bought a cabin that I was restoring in Palo Colorado Canyon, on the northern border of Big Sur. She actually turned out to be about twenty minutes away, out on the cliffs off Spindrift Road. I knew her house, which looked like a little spaceship. We agreed to meet at one p.m. Although she had gained recognition as a Hollywood superstar, I would come to realize just how gifted a painter she was. I was about to find that out and much more.

Giving Kim guitar lessons turned into having me put music to some of her poems. Then we began writing songs together from scratch. A close friendship developed and gradually evolved into an intimate and complex relationship. We spent days walking on the beach below her house, playing primitive marimbas that we would make from tubular bull kelp and driftwood that washed ashore. As Kim jokingly remembers it, we were working on the best ways to get our music out to the public. We came up with the idea of how much fun it would be to do an album of all our songs, and on the cover to have a photo of me chasing after her down the beach, waving a long piece of bull kelp, and her running away yelling, "KELP! KELP!" Days would roll by with Kim attending to her painting and me writing music and playing my guitar.

We were putting together a good library of songs. One of them, "All Roads Pointing Back," was recorded by Harry Belafonte. We formed a music publishing company, Spindrift Music, registered it with the U.S. Copyright Office and joined the BMI music rights organization. My cabin restoration went on hold, and I moved in with Kim.

I was playing gigs in San Francisco and Los Angeles with Bob Dorough. He and I had formed the duo Bob and Al and were signed to a record contract with RCA Records. We were being promoted as jazz's answer to The Everly Brothers. Our single, and the first song I ever wrote, "Walkin' This Road," was selling well and up on the Billboard charts. Side B on that 45 was a song Kim and I had written, "A Train Makes Me Lonely," and it, too, was getting some good radio play.

Playing with Bob in San Francisco was always a blast. Our home base was at the Trident Restaurant on the water in Sausalito, owned by The Kingston Trio, who had just recently recorded a cover of my song. Kim and I would drive up and stop along the way at the old Chicken and Dumplings Diner on US 101, which was Laurel and Hardy's favorite eatery on their drives to and from Los Angeles. The place was loaded with photos of the two of them gorging on big bowls of chicken stew. We would rent a houseboat down on the wharfs for our stay, and I'd sit in at jam sessions on actor Sterling Hayden's old derelict ferryboat, *Sausalito*. We wandered aimlessly around San Francisco, Mill Valley, Mount Tamalpais. No plans, comfortable together, and Kim not burdened with work, feeling at peace with herself.

In the fall of 1963, Kim had to attend to some business matters in Los Angeles. We took our time enjoying the drive down the coast highway and arrived at her Bel Air home away from home in the late evening. The next morning, we were awakened by the phone ringing. Kim answered, and it was her manager telling us to turn on the TV. I got up and turned it on. We were shocked, sitting there on the bed, as we watched Walter Cronkite announce the assassination of President John Fitzgerald Kennedy. November 22, 1963. We were devastated, as was the country, lost in a sudden void. This was beyond politics. The bright aura, the hopes and dreams enveloping the country were suddenly snuffed out.

Kim felt we should find a church and light a candle to honor his life. We drove to a small Catholic sanctuary nearby, knelt in silent prayer, and lit our candle. Here was a bright sunny autumn day, and we were in the City of Angels, but there were no angels that we could find that day. What we needed to find was some open space around us, and we decided to drive up to the planetarium on top of Griffith Park. It wasn't our Big Sur habitat, but the fresh air helped. That day, we shared in the collective grief of everyone around us.

Hollywood was always lurking in the shadows. Kim was excited to be offered the opportunity to work with director Billy Wilder, and although she didn't like her character, Polly, thinking her stupid, and Kim not wanting to feel identified as such, she still agreed to play the role in the film *Kiss Me, Stupid* with Dean Martin and Peter Sellers. Unfortunately, Peter had a heart attack in London, wound up in the hospital, and was replaced by Ray Walston, TV's "My Favorite Martian." Kim went ballistic, storming around the house yelling, "I'm not going to make a film with that martian." Indeed, Peter Sellers would have brought his special brand of humor to the film, and Kim felt she was stuck with the man from Mars.

In order to play the role of Polly, a dumb prostitute, Kim tried to make herself believe that she loved Polly. She was so successful at putting herself into the character that she turned into Polly and brought "stupid Polly" home with her after the movie wrapped. Polly was unable to feel love, and Kim, so wrapped up in the character, was left with emptiness inside. It severely damaged our relationship.

I had just flown back to LA from a concert in New York with Nina Simone. That evening, I knew something was wrong; Kim ignored me and wouldn't communicate. I couldn't reach her and felt it was her way of ending our relationship. Late that night, I packed my belongings, our recording equipment, and with a new crescent moon following me low over the water, I drove up the Pacific Coast Highway to Big Sur, and out of our life together.

We might like to think we're in charge of our destiny, fate, karma, what have you. I laugh. When looking at it, I can see that life happens to us in its own quirky way. Kim never did disappear on me; today, we still remain close friends. I think we're proud of each other and how we've creatively managed our lives.

I've recently composed music for part of a documentary about her, *Kim Novak, The Golden Age Rebel,* in which Kim finds the courage to give up on Hollywood. In one scene, we see her driving up the Pacific Coast Highway to Big Sur and a new way of life, as my guitar is playing her along. *How great is that?*

I MEET BIG SUR LIGHT AND POWER, AND BIG SUR MEETS NINA SIMONE

IN 1970, I WAS LIVING at the old Boronda homestead below Partington Ridge in Big Sur thanks to Walter Trotter, the ranch manager of the Hathaway Ranch. I was doing ranch work for him, while still being able to go off when called to play with Nina.

I had also taken over running the Coast Gallery. It was a gathering place for local artists and craftspeople, and during a party there one Sunday afternoon, a wild bunch of drummers arrived on the deck and put the festivities into high gear. These were not the bottle beaters who normally occasioned the South Coast shindigs. These guys cooked. They had a couple of very basic rhythm guitar players in the group who gave the band some melodic sound, but it called for a hot lead. Feeling inspired to join in, I fired up my amp and started cooking improvised lead lines, and got a few surprised grins from the guys, like "Where did THIS guy come from?" We took off from there. Hello, *Big Sur Light and Power*. The group was mostly based at the De Angulo Ranch on Partington Ridge, where Henry Miller lived, and I was invited to join them there. Being Nina Simone's guitarist and a jazz musician, suddenly finding myself cavorting with a bunch of Big Sur mountain renegades was a totally mind-adjusting experience. Damn, they were raw, but they could play.

It was a communal environment, tending a big organic

garden, living a healthy lifestyle, daily rehearsing and playing on the large open deck they had constructed. Many of their beautiful drums were handmade in Big Sur. I was given a Gibson SG guitar that Jerry Garcia of the Grateful Dead had donated to the band, along with some other instruments and sound equipment.

Jerry's SG was the guitar I used for the Big Sur Light and Power album that we recorded at Pacific High Studios in San Francisco.

At the ranch, we had a generator to power the amps, as there was no electricity on the mountain yet. Eventually, the electric company did supply power poles from the coast highway up the mountain to the entrance of the ranch, and I installed the power lines the rest of the way. Voila! Light and Power.

If I had to define the nature of the group, I think I would call it primal energy, not unlike the drums of Yoruba tribal music that I was introduced to by Baba Olatunji in Nigeria. I must say that Baba's widespread influence on aspiring musicians was profound. Among his inner echelon were Big Sur drummers Gordy Ryan and Steve Loebs, ironically, two non-African Caucasians, who matured into fine musicians, became part of Baba's close-knit family, and today, continue to spread his legacy.

I was at the gallery one day, when the phone rang. It was Nina. "Al," she said, "I'm bored. We have no gigs coming up right now. What do you say I come out for a visit?"

Hmm, Nina Simone in Big Sur? That'll be interesting. "Sure," I said, "when would you like to visit?"

"Right away, where do I book the flight to?"

"Monterey," I said. "Just give me your flight plans and I'll meet your plane."

"Okay, shugga here I come."

The die was cast.

Two days later, Nina arrived, I met her at the airport, and we drove down the coast to Big Sur. On the way, passing through Carmel Highlands, I pointed at Spindrift Road and said, "Kim Novak lives down there. Her house is on the cliffs."

Nina smacked me in the arm and angrily said, "You should have married her. You're a fool."

"Nina," I said, "it was complicated. Our lives were heading in different directions."

"Well, anyways," she said, "you belong to Nina." With that, we drove down that magnificent highway, with Nina oohing and ahhing at the scenery all the way.

I put Nina up at the Big Sur Inn, owned by Helmut (grandpa) Deetjen, an old, surly Norwegian, who was one of the engineers in the 1930s who designed the Monterey and Big Sur section of the Pacific Coast Highway. She was totally awestruck by her little cabin, nestled amongst the giant redwoods.

Nina's visit worked out well. I introduced her to my friend Joel Thomas, who owned the El Matador restaurant in Carmel and was a big fan of hers. They really hit it off, and I could see the beginning of a possible budding romance. One late night, we grabbed a bottle of wine and went down to Esalen Institute, a retreat which, they claim, focuses on building human potential. They have hot mineral spring baths on the cliffs overlooking the Pacific, where, after the paying guests are asleep, the gate guard allows locals to sneak in. We took off our clothes and jumped in for a soak with some wine and candlelight, and Nina was totally in heaven. Nina did spend a bunch of time with Joel, but I sensed it had turned into a budding friendship rather than a romance, and that was just as well. Joel was a tough-living, gambler sort of guy, and I think Nina was neither someone he could continually hang out with, nor cater to her needs. She spent ten days with us. I couldn't remember when I had seen her that relaxed. Her visit came to a close, and she was ready to get back to "civilization," as she put it. "Al, you sure picked a wild place to live in." And indeed I did. The title of a song about Big Sur is "The South Coast the Wild Coast is Calling."

SELMA

March 1965

I WAS APPEARING with Nina Simone at the Village Gate in New York when we were asked by Dr. Martin Luther King to perform at a rally and concert at a seminary in Montgomery, Alabama, for the close of the Selma March for voting rights. This was the third attempt to march and was approved by a federal judge, but for only 300 people. By the last day of the march, the number of people had swelled to over 20,000, and they were being protected by National Guardsmen and the FBI. We decided to go, so Nina, her husband Andrew Stroud, and I flew down to Montgomery on an Eastern Air Lines 707. Upon making our final descent onto the main runway, we saw that it was blocked with sanitation trucks and other vehicles. Governor George Wallace was making sure that no "agitators" could land. The pilot pulled up and announced that we were going to fly on to Jackson, Mississippi.

Upon landing in Jackson, Andy managed to hire a single-engine plane that could land on the small local runway in Montgomery that wasn't being blocked. I got into a four-seater Cessna with Nina and Andy, who was pretty heavy and holding my amp in back. I was up next to the pilot, holding my guitar, when suddenly the nose wheel lifted off the ground and we were sitting back on the tail looking up at the sky as the pilot said in his heavy southern drawl, "Well, we can't take off this a-way." He had Andy and me switch seats, him up forward with the amp and me in back with Nina. The plane slowly settled into its normal position, and off we went.

Andy had made arrangements ahead, and when we landed in Montgomery, a car was waiting and took us to the seminary. As we got out of the car, the local police were blocking the entrance to the soccer field, where the concert was going to be held that night. Nina walked up to one of them and growled, "GET OUTTA MY WAY." Such was Nina's intimidation factor that the seas parted and in we went. We found ourselves in the so-called "backstage" area, where there were two Airstream trailers being used for the artists and dignitaries.

Harry Belafonte's band was standing around the stage. I walked up to the percussionist, Ralph MacDonald, and asked him if he saw any place where I could plug in my amp. He said, "Sure, my brother, come with me," and he led me over to the back of a huge makeshift plywood platform with a curtain scrim around the bottom being used as the stage. He told me to lift the curtain. I did and jumped back in shock. The stage was built on coffins that had evidently been supplied by the black mortuaries in Montgomery. I turned to Ralph, and he was laughing, "Must be a just-in-case kind of deal," he said. Ha, Ha, very funny! I walked back to the trailers, found Nina, and told her what I had just seen. She said, "Shit, they're gonna be for them cracker cops out there."

A little later on, Dr. King arrived and wanted to be introduced to Nina.

She came out of a trailer, and as she walked up to Martin,

yelled out in her North Carolina drawl, "I AINT NON-VIOLENT."

He replied, "That's okay, sister, it's all fine. So good to have you here."

Whereupon Nina stuck out her hand, and switching into her formal semi-British accent said, "I'm so very honored. A pleasure to meet you."

That night at the concert, she was dressed in a pleated plaid skirt, a white long-sleeved shirt, and a knit sleeveless vest that she had been wearing on the trip down. It was so sweet and out of character. She looked like she was right out of prep school as we launched into "Mississippi Goddam," singing it for the first time in front of an audience. Nina had taught it to me just after she wrote it, saying it was her answer for the little girls who were murdered in the church in Birmingham. The crowd went wild and cheered Nina on. Andrew Young said she stole the show with it.

After the concert, we were all taken to a big downtown hotel where two suites were made available for everyone to stay. One for the women and one for the men, probably the first time Black folks had ever been admitted to that hotel. It was an amazing and unforgettable night. I was in the room with Martin, Andrew Young, Harry Belafonte, Leonard Bernstein, Sammy Davis Jr., James Baldwin, Anthony Perkins, Langston Hughes, and Sidney Poitier. The dialogue that went down in the room that night was truly profound, with all of us sitting on the floor talking about the future of the country and how all of what was going on then would reshape the land. I wish I had a recording of it. It would be a treasure. We were told to stay away from the windows and literally sat on the floor all night. In the morning, I snuck a peek out a window through the blinds, and on the rooftops of office buildings, I could see lines of National Guard soldiers standing guard with rifles. *Whoa, so much for reshaping the land,* I thought. *There was still a mountain of work to do.*

The concert was a huge success, but the march was not without tragedy. A Unitarian minister, James Reeb, was attacked, beaten, and died two days later. After the march and the concert, a volunteer from Detroit, Viola Liuzzo, a white mother of five, was shot and killed by the KKK while ferrying marchers back to Selma. And now, fifty-five years later, folks are yelling the rally call, “Black Lives Matter.” Sadly, the beat goes on, the beat goes on.

ON THE ROAD WITH MARTIN

THAT SUMMER after the Selma March, Nina took an extended break from performing. Harry Belafonte heard that I might be available and asked me to join his upcoming tour as lead guitarist for the summer. It sounded good as I was planning to head back to Big Sur, and the tour was going to end at the Greek Theatre in Los Angeles, right down the coast. I joined up with them in Toronto and met his band, among them Ralph MacDonald, Harry's percussionist, who had laughingly shown me the coffins holding up the stage at the rally in Selma.

We were booked into Caesar's Palace in Las Vegas for three weeks, and Dr. King arrived at the end of our engagement to pick up Harry and continue on to San Francisco for a high-roller speaking engagement at the Mark Hopkins Hotel at the top of Nob Hill, one of the most affluent neighborhoods in the country. Harry asked me to go with him and Martin, and bring my little 1907 Washburn guitar that I played when he sang his old field hollers and blues. He said to pack just an overnight bag, including my stage outfit, as we'd be flying in a small Learjet. All my other gear would be brought along with our tour truck to San Francisco for our next engagement.

We boarded the plane around midnight after our show and took off, climbing steeply into a deep, starry night with Martin sitting by a window and me next to him. We were at cruising altitude, Harry was talking with someone, and Martin was looking out the window.

He suddenly turned to me. "Al, look at all those stars. I wonder if there are other souls out there in this universe having to fight for their right to live decently among their brothers and sisters."

I thought about it and said, "Maybe the Green folks don't want to live among the Blue folks. That'd cause some trouble. Whatcha think, Martin, human nature prevails throughout the universe?"

We had a good laugh.

As we were on our approach to San Francisco, the pilot announced that the airport was socked in with fog and we had to join a pattern of flights circling the airport, waiting our turn to land. It was then around one a.m., and we kept circling and circling until the pilot announced that we were running low on fuel. The control tower gave us clearance to use an instrument landing. *Well,* I thought, *we're with Dr. Martin Luther King, so we must have special dispensation from the up high. Yeah, Al, that's reassuring.* Actually, it WAS. The airport was closed, and I could hardly even see the runway lights as we landed. The plane was on a taxiway with the fog so thick we sat there until a security car found us and led us back to the terminal.

The next evening was an elegant Nob Hill black-tie event. We were in Martin's suite with Martin and Harry dressed to the nines in formal attire and me in my "working" attire. Yellow shirt open at the neck Harry-style, grey pants, and black boots.

"Harry, I don't feel comfortable dressed like this."

"Al, you're dressed just fine. You add some color."

I looked at him. "ME? I add color? Whitey adds color?"

Martin, holding back a laugh, put his hand on my shoulder. "Al, you're doing the Lord's work. He doesn't see your clothes; he sees your heart. You just play."

Nothing I could say to that!

The evening was a huge success. Martin was eloquent, charming the rich and famous, wooing them, bringing them into the fold. And he did it so easily, without his usual fire and brimstone. It was really enlightening, hearing him speak with such a different approach. I learned a lot that night about his deep wellspring of knowledge, thoughts, and his understanding of human nature. This was just the beginning of being on the road with Martin.

After Harry's one-week gig in San Francisco, we headed to Seattle, the next stop on our tour. Martin accompanied us, as he was scheduled for a speaking engagement at the University of Washington. We were aboard a United flight, took off on a nice sunny day, and started climbing. Suddenly, the captain announced, "Folks, we just got word that a bomb might be on board, and while this almost never turns out to be true, we have to dump our fuel over the ocean and return to the airport." *Here we go again.*

Harry came back from the first-class section and told us, "Martin has a prayer for these situations, so everybody is covered."

"Man," I shouted, "good thing Martin is with us or we'd be up the creek."

Not everyone was reassured with that, and some of our group were really freaking out.

Martin came back with a smile on his face and cajoled the non-faithful. "Not to worry, the Lord is your shepherd. He's taking care of things right now."

Ralph MacDonald yelled out, "I'm not ready to see him just yet."

Martin said, "Neither am I, but we talk together all the time, don't you?"

We landed safely, and the plane was directed to a remote part of the airport. We were hustled off the plane and greeted by a bomb squad and FBI agents, who announced that they were going to search the plane and our luggage. That didn't go over too well with some of us in the band.

Ralph went up to one of the agents and said, "My man, we have an awkward situation here. If you just, by accident, happen to find some weed in our luggage, does that mean trouble?"

The agent laughed and said, "We're not interested in your private belongings, just bombs. You're cool." Ralph turned around and yelled, "God bless America!"

PARIS AND STOCKHOLM

March 28th and March 31st, 1966

WE FLEW INTO PARIS with Martin for a fundraiser and concert at Palais des Sports organized by the French actors Yves Montand, Simone Signoret, and their organization, *The Franco-American Committee of Support for Racial Integration.* The speech Martin gave that night was directed toward one's heart. He spoke of our sameness, our common idiosyncrasies, fears, love of family; elements in humanity that make people more like our own self than we sometimes care to see. The common fiber of mankind, regardless of race, color, or religion making the human spirit one body under God. His talk that night was like a sermon, loving, so different from the fiery political speeches I heard from him back home.

The mood in Stockholm two days later was very festive. We performed at the Opera House, reached by walking over a canal on a bridge lit with huge flaming torches; how it might have looked in the time of the ancient Vikings. Martin's speech was again like a sermon, loving, gently reaching out to his flock, but at the same time driving home the sense of purpose needed to bring about change in the human condition. He spoke of how we need to focus on poverty and education regardless of color. Harry and I ended the evening and our journey with his trademark calypso, "Matilda," with the audience joining in.

Flying home, I was overwhelmed with the feeling that I was

a participant in a resounding moment in history. The impact of Martin's crusade was astounding. On the flight, I had a chance to sit with him for a moment and share some of my thoughts.

He looked at me and said, "Al, you're realizing the big picture. It's larger than any one of us, and from this point forward, it cannot be deterred. Not by the politicians, and certainly not by the racists. The people have raised their voices." He laughed and said, "Al, you're an important player in this army's marching band."

I went back to my seat and thought, so now I'm in Martin's Marching Band. A guitar in a marching band? Well, I don't play a bugle or a drum, guess I'll just have to keep on marching with my guitar.

❄ ❄ ❄

Houston, Texas, October 17th, 1967

I was with Harry Belafonte and the band. We arrived with Martin to hold a fundraiser and concert at the Sam Houston Coliseum. Our featured artist was going to be Aretha Franklin. I looked forward to backing her up, but I felt uneasy about this one. Houston had a history of racial problems, and we were told that Klansmen had distributed hate messages on downtown sidewalks. Still, the mood was upbeat, and we were expecting over 4,000 people to attend. Martin was not at all concerned about a disturbance.

The performance began with Harry introducing the evening. We played a set, and then he brought on Aretha, and suddenly, during one of her songs, foul-smelling smoke was blowing through the hall. People yelled and started for the exits. Martin jumped up to the microphone and told the crowd, "We have problems here tonight. The forces of evil are always around us, but we will not be deterred. Just stay put, and we'll clear the air." The management did clear it out, the crowd stayed, and Aretha continued on with her performance.

Martin was his eloquent self when he took the stage, lashing out against our involvement in the Vietnam War. He spoke about recommitting himself to bringing *Operation Breadbasket* to the city, his program to encourage businesses with substantial Black patronage to hire more Black workers. He closed the evening with his memorable speech, "We are going to build right here a nation where men and women, black and white, Jew and gentile, Protestant and Catholic, will stand together and sing the words of that old Negro spiritual, "Free at last. Free at last. Thank God almighty, we're free at last."

This, just six months before he would be gunned down in Memphis, where he had gone to support striking garbage workers.

NINA AND THE PRIME MINISTER OF BARBADOS

"HI, SHUGGA." It was Nina on the phone from Barbados. We had an upcoming gig in New York, and I was wondering when she would get in touch.

"I'm not going to play the show if you don't come down here to rehearse."

"Nina," I said, "you always say that, and when I get there, we never rehearse. You just want me to take you dancing or shopping."

"Al, I promise that we'll rehearse. I have a small piano here at this beautiful plantation house, Old Trees, on the beach, that the prime minister of Barbados set me up in. Please, come down for a few days. It'll be good for you, and we'll go back up to New York together."

Hooked again. "Okay," I said, "I'll catch a flight out of JFK, day after tomorrow."

"Wonderful!" she said. "When you get here, just have a taxi take you to Old Trees. Everyone knows where it is."

Done. I booked a flight on BIWI Air, packed a few things in a carry-on, and got down to JFK. The flight was uneventful; I grabbed a taxi outside the terminal and asked the driver if he knew where Old Trees was. "Sure-thing, mister, hop in." The drive was great; the breeze flowing through the windows was an ambrosia of flowers. Ahh, Nina was right.

Arriving at Old Trees, the house was wide open. I looked

around and no Nina. The house was a tropical mansion, complete with pillars. I walked out from the veranda onto the beach, and looking out to sea, I noticed a spot moving through the water. I mean, I was looking way out to sea. The spot grew larger, and larger, as it came toward shore. AH-HA! Nina, my Pisces sister. Nina was a fantastic swimmer and could have made the Olympic team. She sauntered up, out of the water, and yelled, "I hope you brought a bathing suit." She ran up and gave me a big wet hug and one of her famous smooches.

"Okay, Nina," I said, "you win, this is great."

She showed me my room, we relaxed, we sat out under the trees, and caught up with each other. Dinner that night was at a small kiosk down the beach, wonderful fresh fish, served at tables among the trees. We walked back to the house along the beach, and I must say, I had seldom seen Nina this peaceful.

Two days later, Nina told me that she didn't feel safe. There were robberies in the area, and she would appreciate my changing the lock on the entrance door by the driveway. I said, "Sure." She took me into the village where we bought a new lock. Then told me she needed to do some shopping, and would I find my way back by myself and fix the lock. "No problem," I said, and off I went.

I went about replacing the lock, and I was removing the tumbler when a black Town Car pulled up in the driveway. A man got out of the passenger side, leaving the driver in the car.

"Hello there," he said. "Who are you, and what are you doing?"

"As you can see," I said, "I'm changing the lock for my friend."

"I see . . . that would be Miss Simone, I would assume."

"Yes," I said, "she's away shopping. Should I say who called?"

"Please, if you would be so kind, just say that Errol called." And with that he returned to the car and off they went.

When Nina returned, I told her that Errol had come by while she was away. She laughed and said, "Oh, he's my new fling. He invited me to a reception the prime minister is holding at Sam Lord's Castle. Sam Lord was an old pirate. You'll love it. You'll be my escort, and you might meet Errol. He's very British."

"Nina, I don't have clothes for this kind of shindig."

"Nonsense," she said. "Run into town and pick up some things. It's very informal. You have a jacket, just get a shirt and tie."

Oh well, I thought, *go with the flow, Al, it could be fun.*

That evening, we called for a taxi and were delivered to a setting out of an old Errol Flynn pirate movie. We were ushered into a large hall by a butler in a swashbuckling outfit and were led to a reception line. Nina whispered to me, "Al, looks like it's a party for some foreign dignitaries. You'll have to say, how do you do, so nice to meet you. You know, that kind of stuff. You'll meet the prime minister."

"Sure, Nina." And off we went.

The line moved right along, I was meeting this envoy, that ambassador, the prime minister's wife, and after a bit, I came to the prime minister himself. "OH NO," I said.

"Oh yes," he said. "We meet again, my friend." It was Errol, Errol Barrow, the prime minister of Barbados. He laughed and said, "Just like our Nina, having a little fun at our expense, changing the lock at my getaway cottage. Please be at ease, no hard feelings."

I introduced myself, and he said we would chat later, and we did. I told him about my work with Nina, and he said that he had many of her records. He was very nice, very gracious, and yes, very British. Nina came up to us, and said, "So, you two have met." Errol and I looked at each other and shook our heads. Nina giggled.

The rest of my stay was really nice and relaxing. No calamities had intruded on this tropical paradise . . . A few days later, Nina and I packed up, and headed to the airport. On the flight home, Nina said, "I'm in love with Errol. I don't imagine I can do anything about it, but I'll just ride the wave until it hits the beach."

I always noticed that Nina kept a framed, signed photograph of Errol on her mantel or desk, wherever she was living. Indeed, the lady had fallen in love. A few years later, Nina was distraught upon learning that Errol had passed. In a concert, she paused before beginning her first song and said, "This concert is dedicated to my true love, Errol Barrow. May he rest in peace."

MIDNIGHT AT CARNEGIE HALL

June 27, 1977

NINA HAD BEEN studying and performing the music of Kurt Weill and Berthold Brecht. When George Wein, the founder of the Newport Jazz Festival, approached her about appearing at Carnegie Hall as an adjunct to the festival; she proposed performing a Weill and Brecht concert. I would be her accompanist along with the Brooklyn Philharmonia Orchestra under the direction of her friend Lukas Foss. This sounded like it could be a grand New York event, and George planned for it to be held at midnight. We would be interpreting works from *Threepenny Opera*, *Mahogany*, and various other pieces from the Weill and Brecht repertoire. *Wow,* I thought, *Nina is biting off quite a bit, having to embody a large chunk of music, and having only previously performed a small number of their songs.* I spoke with Nina about the short amount of time to prepare, and she agreed it was a tall order, but she was confident that she could do it. We had a rehearsal the day before in a practice hall, which went well, but I felt that Nina was a bit tentative with her music.

The day of the concert arrived, and a rehearsal and sound check were scheduled for that afternoon on the Carnegie stage. Nina was staying at a hotel across town on East Fifty-Seventh Street. Carnegie Hall is on West Fifty-Seventh at the corner of Seventh Avenue, with the stage entrance around the corner on West Fifty-Sixth. The front entrance was always closed, and doors did not open until the performance. There was a Ticketron kiosk selling Broadway theatre tickets in a corner of the landing outside the front doors, but it had nothing to do with Carnegie Hall. Nina was to be driven to the stage entrance for the rehearsal, but as I later learned, had decided to walk, stopping along the way to browse the fine boutiques on Fifty-Seventh Street. She left the hotel early without telling anyone of her plans. The car arrived at the hotel, and when the driver phoned up to her room and there was no answer, he inquired at the desk and was told that Miss Simone was seen leaving earlier.

Back at the Hall, we ran the arrangements with the orchestra, although Nina had not shown up. The music was coming together nicely, and we finished the rehearsal without her. George Wein was concerned. I phoned the hotel and was told she was not in. I left a message for her and told George that I would stay on it.

He was nervous and said, "Al, maybe I shouldn't have done this, but at rehearsal yesterday, Nina asked for her entire fee up front . . . and I gave it to her."

"George, no!" I said.

"Yes," he said. "She assured me that we had worked well together for quite a while, and she had always honored her performances. She said this was the beginning of our collaborating on a higher level than just playing at my Storyville club in Boston and appearing at my Newport Jazz Festivals. Al, she was so seductive, and she got me."

Oh boy, I said to myself, Nina on the loose with fifteen grand? *Hold on, Alvin, here we go.* I told George that Nina most often did not attend rehearsals, all the while really concerned that this was a different kettle of fish. This was one rehearsal that Nina really did need. The music was intricate, and at times she would be away from the security of her piano, standing downstage with the orchestra backing her.

I left the Hall, went outside around to the front, saw the kiosk, and went up and inquired about Nina. Evidently, Nina had arrived at the front entrance on Fifty-Seventh Street, tried the doors, and to her dismay, they, of course, were locked. She had gone over to the front of the line at the kiosk and told the man selling tickets that she was Nina Simone, was here for the rehearsal, and to open the door. He said that he was not with Carnegie Hall, didn't have a key, and that she should go around the corner to the stage entrance. The man said that Nina was outraged, yelling that she was being discriminated against because she was Black, that she was Nina Simone and would not go around back like some kitchen maid. The man said he was trying to sell tickets and she was causing a disturbance, and he told her to leave or he would call the police. With that, she cussed him out and left. *Uh oh, the fuse had been lit. She didn't remember the stage entrance?* The Carnegie Hall stage entrance was world renowned. It was quite an accomplishment to walk through that door as an artist, and Nina had been through that door before. Go figure.

It was then six o'clock. I phoned over to Nina's hotel and was told there was a "do not disturb" on her phone. *Okay,* I thought, *at least that's something.* I had a quick dinner, then went to my room, dressed for this formal black-tie evening, and decided I'd best get over to Nina's hotel and see what was up. I was staying at the Park Sheraton Hotel, across from Carnegie Hall. I went out, took a taxi over to Nina's hotel, and went up to the desk.

"Excuse me," I said, "I'm with Nina Simone. She's a guest here, and I tried to reach her, but her phone was blocked."

"Just a moment," the desk person said. He came back a moment later and said, "I'm sorry, sir, but Miss Simone checked out a while ago and didn't leave any forwarding information."

Oh no, I thought, *the drama begins, and now I have to tell George.* I went on to Carnegie Hall, trying to get into Nina's head. What could she be thinking, messing with George Wein? He put up more than just Nina's fee. He booked the hall, did the promotion, hired the orchestra. You won't find anyone more straight-arrow than George. What was she up to?

I got to the Hall, and it was now nine o'clock. Everyone would be there soon, and I had to try to figure out where Nina was, and knowing Nina, I was already thinking that she wouldn't show.

George arrived a short time later with his lovely wife, Joyce, and they immediately bore down on me. He said, "Al, have you heard from Nina? The limo is ready to pick her up."

"George," I said, "we'd better sit down. Nina checked out of her hotel a couple of hours ago with no forwarding info."

"Oh my god," he said. "What are we going to do?"

The clock was ticking, midnight was approaching, and the crowd would soon be arriving. Would Nina surprise us and show up? Having been through these dramas before, I didn't hold out much hope.

"George, first, let's try and see if we can track her down. I think that if she's on the run, she'll try and get out of town with her money. I mean your money."

George held his head; Joyce just shook hers.

"She flew in from Geneva, but I think maybe she might try and get to Barbados. She mentioned something about having an affair with the prime minister and might head there. If that's the case, the only way out tonight might be with a flight out of JFK airport."

I was right, except there were no flights out that night. I found that she was booked on a British West Indies Airways flight, popularly known as BIWI, the next morning. That meant she had to be staying at a motel by the airport. I started phoning the motels around JFK with no luck, and then BINGO! She was booked into a Howard Johnson's Motor Lodge near the airport.

Ten o'clock, with time ticking. We were all standing around the phone backstage. At least we had something solid to work with, but how to get Nina to change her mind? George decided to send his wife, Joyce, and their associate, Darlene Chan, out to the motel in the limo. When she got there, she would phone us, and I would then phone Nina's room, talk to her and try to find out what prompted her to run. I would tell Nina that Joyce was outside with the limo. Joyce would then knock on Nina's door and tell her that she was there to help her, and they would drive back together.

We waited. Joyce was on her way, and in thirty minutes, the drama would continue.

"Do you think Nina will change her mind?" George asked me.

"The gods only know, George," I said. "I think, in any

case, you should prepare a statement for the audience if she doesn't show."

"What can I tell them, besides refunding their ticket?" he said.

"That's a tough one, this is a New York crowd. They don't easily forgive and forget. They love Nina but are wise to her antics and won't be happy."

We waited, and then the phone rang. Joyce and Darlene were there at the motel, but while waiting in the hallway at Nina's door, a security guard came up to them, thinking they were prostitutes working the hotel, and Joyce explained the situation. I told Joyce that when she heard Nina's phone ring, to wait a bit so that I could speak with Nina, then knock on the door and announce herself. Nina knew Joyce and liked her, which might help. Now it was my turn. I rang the motel and was put through to Nina's room.

"What!" she said.

"Sweetheart, it's me," I said.

Very softly, she said, "Hello, Al. I'm free now."

"Nina," I said, "your loving fans are back at Carnegie Hall awaiting what promises to be your triumphant performance with a symphony orchestra. I'll be right there with you. This is something you have always wanted to achieve, and at Carnegie Hall. Please come back. Joyce is right outside, ready to assist you."

At that moment, I heard Joyce knock at the door announcing herself. Nina went to the door, leaving the phone open, and I could hear Joyce trying to coax Nina.

"Nina," she said. "I have the limo. Let's drive back and have some champagne along the way. We'll have a terrific night."

"No, Joyce," she said, "it's over now. Tell George I'm so sorry, but I'm leaving the United Snakes of America and all its racism. Please leave."

Nina came back to the phone and again, very quietly, said, "It's over, Al. I'm free now. I'm gone." And she hung up the phone.

I hung up. Joyce phoned back, and I told her it was no use, that when Nina was in this space, there was no reversing it. George got on the phone and told Joyce to come back, and then he sat down to prepare something to confront the crowd with. I apprised Lukas Foss of the situation, and sadly, he dismissed the orchestra. By then, the audience was arriving in the hall. We waited until everyone was seated, and with a heavy heart, George went out.

The shockwave throughout the hall, I'm sure, must have loosened the plaster. The hall was abuzz with groans and conversation. The crowd mostly sat for a while and then slowly made their way out of the hall and onto West Fifty-Seventh Street. The overflow spilled out into the roadway, and people were greeting each other left and right. "Hey, it's been years, what have you been up to?" and "Another Nina Simone evening. Shoulda' known." But, strangely enough, the mood was festive out there on the street. Go figure.

As I was putting away my guitar backstage, George and Joyce came up to me and said they were going to have a little postmortem gathering at their place, and would I come join them.

We sat around talking about what might have been and

had a couple of drinks. George walked over to his piano, he being a pretty darn good piano player himself, and said, "Al, get out your guitar. Let's at least leave this evening with some music." I sat down next to him. He looked at me and said, "This should be appropriate." We played the blues.

EXCERPT FROM LETTER FROM NINA SIMONE

April 4, 1977

Regarding upcoming Carnegie Hall Weill/Bertolt Brecht program

Still working very slowly and DEEPLY on "3 Penny" and Mahagonny. My heart is there. Need more time to work on it—that's all. Nothing's changed in that direction. A whole bit in this week's Newsweek on WEILL/BRECHT. You should get it.

❄ ❄ ❄

EXCERPT FROM LETTER FROM NINA SIMONE

June 6, 1977

Concert's scaring me now. Because of lack of coordinated practice and whatever. This thing is between you and me. Will practice more Brecht.

TROUBLE IN MIND

THROUGH THE MANY YEARS that I accompanied Nina Simone both on and off the stage, I was fiercely protective of her private life and mental struggles. This was true, as well, for our close inner sanctum of friends and band members. She belonged to us, and we belonged to her.

I am reluctant even now, eighteen years after Nina's passing, to share the facts of her struggle with mental illness, which have been so misconstrued by the media and the public. Yet I feel an obligation to share Nina's battle with her demons, in the belief that this will help the reader and her many fans to understand Nina Simone more fully and compassionately. The following recollections are meant to enlighten and gain a deeper understanding of Nina's emotional roller coaster, and her evolution from seemingly odd and eccentric, to full-blown raging disconnects.

Summer 1958: Looking back at the evening of my first meeting with Nina, I see now that her behavior was very odd. As I mentioned, I was standing on the little stage at the Bucks County Playhouse Inn, having tuned my guitar, and had not yet met Nina. She came up onto the stage, sat down, and without acknowledging my presence, never looking at me, and as though she were there alone, began playing her Bach introduction to the song "Little Girl Blue." *Hello, Nina?* I thought. *Your guest, whom you have never met before, is standing four feet from you.* Looking at it now, I realize that I had to play myself into her realm, make her accept me through my playing, or she would have totally ignored my existence. I later learned that she had never before played with another musician. Even so, what a strange encounter to have with a fellow artist.

It was as early as 1960, while playing with Nina at the Village Gate, that I was beginning to have concerns over her emotional well-being, her relationships, and erratic behavior. She was attracting a group of unsavory lesbian "toughs," who seemed to be trying to control her. The band at that time included bassist Chris White, drummer Bobby Hamilton, and me—Nina's backbone band during this period.

One afternoon, my phone rang. It was one of the lesbian women.

"You don't need to come to the performance tonight. You've been fired," she said.

"Oh," I said, "does this come from Miss Simone?"

"This comes from her new management team," she said. "We've decided that Miss Simone doesn't need a guitar player."

"Well, thanks for letting me know. I wouldn't want to waste an evening."

I hung up, not even considering what had just transpired. That evening, as usual, I showed up for the gig at The Gate, went back to the dressing room, and Nina hadn't yet arrived. I hung out with Chris and Bobby, never mentioning my phone conversation from that afternoon. It came time for the band to go on. We played a few songs, and then Nina was announced. "Ladies and gentlemen, the Village Gate is proud to present the High Priestess of Soul, Miss Nina Simone." I was standing toward the front of the stage, in the curve of the piano. Nina came on stage to the crowd's applause, passed in front of me with no acknowledgment, sat down at the piano, and we went into a swinging rendition of "Just in Time." During the set, Nina introduced the band, including me, the guitar player who had been fired that afternoon.

We finished the set and went off into the dressing room. The burly new management team was there, looking like security guards, not saying a word, and Nina called for her champagne. It was delivered by a nervous young waiter named Sam, who would in a few years be the acclaimed playwright and actor, Sam Shepard. Oddly, the matter of my firing was never brought up, and I think that possibly Nina didn't even know about it. This was typical of situations from which Nina would have to extricate herself. I had no idea how Nina had gotten involved with these women. Shortly after they had disappeared from her circle. I realized that I would have to be on guard in the future, of people who might take advantage of Nina for their own self-interest.

Early 1970s: Nina agreed to do a weekend at Upstairs at the Village Gate and asked me to do the gig with her. Three nights, just the two of us. I hadn't seen her for a while and was concerned when, in the midst of rehearsing some new material, she suddenly jumped up from the piano and started ranting about everyone stealing from her. Record companies stealing her royalties, and accusing her sister, Francis, and brother, Sam, of stealing from her. I had no idea what was going on in her mind. Her sister, Lucille, and her father, John Waymon, had recently passed away within two weeks of each other, and maybe Nina was really struggling with it.

She had gone down to Tryon, North Carolina, to be with her family, but she refused to attend her father's funeral. I know she had a deep rift with him. Nina once told me that she was angry with him because he claimed he was the breadwinner for the family, but it was really her mother, Mary Kate, who supported them. Though I think her rift with him went deeper than that.

I couldn't calm her down that night. She began yelling at me, saying that I was weak. What? What was she talking about? Weak about what? That ended our rehearsal.

At the gig the next night, the room was packed, her close friend, James Baldwin (Jimmie), was in the audience, and I was looking forward to a nice evening of music, hoping to put aside my concerns about Nina's outburst the previous day. Our first set was to begin at 8:30 p.m. I was sitting with Jimmie at his table, and it was nearing time for our set to begin. I went into the dressing room to await Nina, who, as of nine p.m., hadn't shown up yet.

Nina stormed through the doors, went right up to the stage, and started yelling about the Israelis killing the Palestinians and American Jews treating Black folks like slaves. Art D'Lugoff, the Village Gate's owner, Jewish and also in the audience, and whose wife is Israeli, yelled out to her, "Nina, there's no need to act this way . . . we're all friends here."

Jimmie, sensing doomsday, ran up on stage and said, "Nina, I haven't seen you in ages, aren't you going to sing to me?"

Nina, totally taken by surprise, rushed over to him, and said, "Dahling, it's so good to see you, of course, Nina's going to sing for you. You're going to sit right up here with me." She sat down at the piano, and Jimmie sat at the piano with her.

The storm passed, and the audience, who stayed, in spite of her outburst, indeed enjoyed a fine evening of music. But I came away from that evening seeing that the storm within Nina was growing worse.

One time, during a concert, a fly landed on the piano in front of Nina. She turned to the audience and said, "My father is here tonight." Nina would continue to say this whenever a fly would land near her, or say, "My father is listening." This alarmed me, and I tried to figure out how I could possibly approach Nina to see if she would agree to speaking with a counselor, but that was years before she seriously sought help.

July 1977

Nina had flown to Barbados after skipping out of her Carnegie Hall concert in June. She spent around a week in Barbados and then returned home to Switzerland. She phoned to remind me that we had two concerts coming up and that I should first come to her house for rehearsal. She never mentioned the disaster at Carnegie Hall. I flew into Geneva to meet with her and prepare for the concerts at the North Sea Jazz Festival in Holland and the Antibes Jazz Festival in Juan Les Pins, France, later that month. George Wein was still willing to book her for the Antibes Festival, amazingly, since she stiffed him by not showing up for the Carnegie Hall concert that he had promoted.

It was fairly early in the morning. Nina was standing by her little aging yellow Renault outside the terminal. When she saw me, she ran up, gave me a huge hug, big smooch, and off we went to her home in Trélex, a village outside of Nyon.

"Al, there's so much to tell you," she said as we drove along. "My friend, Berenice, you'll meet her . . . she's Swiss and a top executive with the Swiss subsidiary of an American car company. She's a lesbian, very beautiful, and I think she's in love with me. She found my house for me and has really helped with getting settled in."

We arrived at a very nice-looking modern home situated in a small open development in the countryside, with a view out toward mountains in the distance. Nina showed me my bedroom and told me to make myself at home.

"Help yourself to food in the kitchen," she said. "I'm going to have a nap, and this evening I'm taking you out to a disco in Geneva. Everybody knows me there, and we'll have a blast."

"Nina," I said, "You told me on the phone that I should come to you in Geneva early instead of meeting you in Holland so that we could rehearse some new songs for the festivals."

She laughed. "Al, you know as well as me, that you and I do not have to rehearse. We're fantastic when we improvise together, all fresh and spontaneous."

I couldn't argue with that. Together we did create some powerful music that way, not to disparage a rousing rehearsal, which at times would reveal her as a stringent taskmaster. She went off to bed. Hungry, I headed off to see what I might find in the kitchen.

I went to the fridge, opened it, and recoiled in shock, holding my nose. On a shelf, sitting on a plate, was a slab of green mold that looked like it might have once been beef liver.

Sitting beside it was what was once bread, also covered in green mold. There was a withered apple . . . and I don't think I need to describe the rest. It looked and smelled like a dumpster, not a fridge. This was Nina on her own, not taking care of herself, probably spending too much money eating out. This was worrisome. Nina was just getting back on her feet after being quite broke, as promoters stopped booking her because of her volatility or failure to appear. I went to my bedroom and lay down, wondering what was in store for an evening out with Nina.

Later that day, I awoke to a gentle shake of my shoulder, and there was Nina smiling down at me. "Hi, Shugga, time to move. We're having dinner at the Hotel Clos du Sadex on Lake Geneva in Nyon. It's a beautiful old mansion and very exclusive. I eat there all the time. I want them to meet you. They love me, and I'm allowed to run a tab, so we won't need any money. After dinner, we'll drive into Geneva."

Yikes, I thought, *this sounds expensive . . . I wonder how much of a tab Nina has run up? I think I'd better be prepared to pay for dinner. Maybe I can quietly speak with the management and find out just how much she owes.*

We arrived at the hotel, and Nina introduced me to the maître d' and staff using her royal British accent. We were then led into a very elegant dining room with a view looking out onto Lake Geneva. Dinner was excellent and included a very fine bottle of Bordeaux and a brandy with our coffee. This dinner was adding up. Nina excused herself to visit the ladies' room, which gave me an opportunity to speak with the maître d'.

I discreetly inquired as to Nina's outstanding bill and was told that she had actually stayed there for a few weeks when she first arrived in Switzerland. Nina had told them that her banker would contact them regarding payment, which, as of now, had not been settled. The total bill came to over $7,000 US, not including that night's dinner, which I told them I would cover. It alone came to over $300. I told them that I would contact the banker, and I returned to the table. Nina asked for another brandy, I paid the bill, and we said our goodbyes. *Who,* I thought, *is this banker, Nina?*

We were then off to Geneva and the disco, Nina insisting that she was fine to drive, and what a drive it was. As we neared town, the traffic was down to a crawl, and as we passed a park with a broad tree-lined promenade along the road, Nina hopped the curb, drove through the trees so we were driving on the walkway, trees on our left and park benches on our right.

Horrified, I said, "Nina! What are you doing? You're going to get us arrested, there are people here!"

"Not to worry, Al, they'll get out of the way." And she began laughing and honking her horn.

This was not the responsible driver of a few years ago, who would drive me around New York City in her Mercedes convertible. This was manic. I had never seen this level of erratic behavior in Nina. We continued on until I saw a red traffic light down the road and suggested we rejoin the traffic.

"Al, you're such a spoilsport," she said, but she drove back through the trees and wormed her way into the line of cars.

The disco was upstairs in a Fabrique, an old, converted

factory. There was a line waiting to get in. Nina took me by the hand and led me past the crowd to the ticket entrance, where we were greeted by a bouncer-type security guy in women's makeup. He obviously knew her, gave Nina a big hello, and waved us through. We walked into a large, smoke-filled dance floor, a long bar down the far end, and a DJ holding forth on a stage. The music was deafening, and the strobe lighting was psychedelic. There was a second level overlooking the dance floor, with tables lined against the walls. The whole scene was right out of Studio 54 in New York City. Nina was obviously ready to boogie, pulled me over to the bar, where she was greeted by the bartender, also in makeup, whom she knew by name, and ordered a bottle of Dom Perignon.

"Nina," I said, "a bottle of Dom Perignon is going to cost a fortune at this place."

"Al, you always forget who you're with. Nina Simone doesn't have to pay at places like this."

The bartender returned, set our glasses, popped the cork, and poured.

"A votre sante," Nina said, and downed her drink.

"Sante, Nina," I said, "but let's take it easy. It could be a long night."

She laughed at me and pulled us out onto the dance floor.

The evening moved along. Some people she had previously met at the club arrived. Nina introduced us and ordered more champagne for everyone. Another toast to whatever . . . I was now really wondering about not having to pay, and then they all went out to the dance floor. I remained at the bar. I needed to know what Nina was up to with running large tabs that she couldn't afford, and using some mysterious, and possibly fictitious, banker as her intermediary.

"Excuse me," I said to the bartender, who was fluent in English. "Are Nina's drinks on the house?"

"Just a moment," he said. "I'll get our manager, and he can fill you in."

The manager came over, we introduced ourselves to each other, and I asked him about Nina's running tab.

"Miss Simone opened an account with us," he said, "which she is making arrangements for her banker to pay. We normally ask for a deposit, but since it is Nina Simone, we waived it. Frankly, we're becoming somewhat concerned, as we have not received any payments as yet."

Just as I thought. Nina was using her name to get by without paying her bills.

"Can you give me the name of her banker?" I asked. "I'll look into the delay."

"Of course," he said. He excused himself, came back a few minutes later, and gave me the banker's information. I suggested that he put a hold on her account until they received payment. He agreed, and told the bartender to stop running Nina's tab.

Nina and her friends came back to the bar. She was having a great time, and I'm sure her friends were enjoying the free drinks, with none of them offering to buy a round. Typical of some of the types of people that Nina's vulnerability could attract.

Nina called for another round of drinks, switching to

brandy for herself. The bartender brought the drinks and asked everyone for payment, saying that drinks were no longer to be put on Nina's account. Nina hit the ceiling, began yelling at the bartender, and wanted to see the manager. I told Nina that I had spoken with him, and he was concerned that they had yet to receive payment from her banker. She flew into a rage, telling me I should keep out of her business, screamed obscenities, threw her glass at the bartender. I grabbed her and said, "Nina, I think we should get out of here. They might call the police. The Swiss tend to be very conservative people, and do not tolerate rowdiness."

"Let's go, Al," she said. "This place is just trying to use me for my name, and I don't need their shit."

We pushed through the crowd and got out to the street. She said she was too angry to drive and gave me the keys to the car. Amen for that, not a good idea for her to get behind the wheel. Nina calmed down on the way home and talked about taking me to a spa that she frequented in the mountains.

I asked her about her banker, and she said, "Oh yes, Dominic Dunant. He's an executive at a private bank. You will have to meet him. He pays my bills. He's wonderful, I think he's afraid of me and does whatever I tell him to do." *Sure he does, Nina,* I thought. He pays your bills with what money? When we had arrived home, Nina bid me goodnight and went to bed, leaving me wondering what was coming tomorrow.

Yes, I definitely had to meet Dominic the banker, and I'd better be prepared for the worst. I awoke the next morning to a cacophony of jingling bells and thought I was back on the farm

Al and Raymond Gonzalez paying our dues.

Nina and Al arriving for Antibes Jazz Festival.

Al with Harry Belafonte.

The A team. Nina's long-time support group. (L/R) Gerrit Debruin, Raymond Gonzalez, Paul Robinson, Al, Roger Nupie.

Above: Nina having breakfast in bed at Hotel in Antibes.

Below: Kim Novak painting in her studio.

Nina and Al toasting concert in Lebanon. Photo by Julie Skarrett.

Left: Nina ad for Apollo theater 1961. See P. 54.

Below: Nina and Al at the Village Gate 1973.

Nina Simone Band. (L/R) Paul Robinson, drums; Leopoldo Fleming, percussion; Al, guitar; Chris White, bass. Photo by Julie Skarrett.

Miss NINA SIMONE
will NOT perform
TONIGHT (Wed.)
instead she will be in
MONTGOMERY, ALA.
helping to make a little history (along with her husband, Andy Stroud, musician Al Schackman and Art D'Lugoff).

Above: Going to Selma march.

Right: Nina fishing on Lake Geneva, Switzerland.

Above: Nina with band and officers and crew of the HMS Intrepid. She was named the ship's mascot. Below left: Bruce Langhorne. Below right: Nina and Al with Pete Townshend of The Who.

Above: Nina with James Baldwin.

Left: Al with Robert Redford at Sundance Film Festival attending Netflix documentary premier *What Happened Miss Simone?*
Below: Midnight at Carnegie Hall.
See P. 118.

Above: Backstage with my children at Boston Pops. L-R: Steffan, Davi, Aurin, Nina, Al, Kris. Below: Olympia theater, Paris.

when I was a kid. It was a line of cows being walked toward the mountains. The lead cow was wearing a bell that must have been two feet long, and the others were all wearing smaller ones. Nina was standing in the living room looking out the windows. She turned and said, "Look, Al, they are taking the cows up into the mountains. It's so peaceful living here in Switzerland."

Wonderful, I thought. It wasn't so peaceful last night.

Nina said, "Today, I want to take you up the mountain to my spa. You'll be able to see how well I'm taken care of here."

"Great," I said, "but first, I really need to meet Mr. Dunant at the bank. I need to know how well you're being taken care of financially. If you want me to relax and enjoy being here, please, let's go and see him."

"Al, you're such a worrywart. Okay, I'll phone him and see if he can meet with us today, and then you're mine."

Nina phoned him, and he was able to meet with us in the afternoon. We arrived at the bank, were ushered into his office, and Nina introduced us. Dominic was younger than I had imagined. He appeared to be a conservative and mild-mannered person, very gracious. A nice guy. We sat down together, coffee was brought, and we talked about Nina's forthcoming concerts and setting up in her new home. At one point, I had to get to the crux of things.

"Mr. Dunant," I said, "is Miss Simone's account being handled by you personally?"

A sudden chill crept into the air.

"It is rather complicated," he said. "Miss Simone's account in New York was closed, and we are trying to reestablish it here."

I suddenly realized that I'd better not proceed any further in front of Nina.

"That's fine," I said. "It's good to know that Nina is in capable hands."

We spoke for a while longer, and then it was clear that it was time to leave. I shook hands with Mr. Dunant. He gave me his card and said to call anytime.

We left his office, and I said, "Nina, how rude of me. I didn't give Mr. Dunant my card. I'll be right back." And with that, turned and abruptly went back into his office. Mr. Dunant and I quickly became "Al" and "Dominic."

"Al," he said, "thank God you came back. I do not know what to do. I am frantic. Nina has put me in an impossible situation. I am getting calls from everywhere, people under the impression that I am her solicitor and demanding payment for accounts owed by Nina that she forwards to me for payment. She has no funds, and the bank cannot give her a loan without collateral, of which she has none. I have personally loaned her some money, but nothing that comes close to settling the bills she is running up. I cannot do any more."

"We'll work through this. Nina has two concerts coming up this month, and I'll see that she deposits her earnings for you to manage, if you are willing."

"Yes, of course," he said. "I'm a big fan of Nina, and I want to help. Heaven knows, she needs help. Please let me know as soon as possible, and I'll try to 'hold down the fort' as they say in America."

With that, I gave him my card, and we shook hands again. I told him I was staying with Nina and he could reach me there.

I walked out to the lobby, and as we were leaving, Nina said proudly, "You see, Al? How I was treated in the bank? That's the way Nina Simone is treated in Europe. Not like in the United Snakes of America."

On the way home, Nina told me that we were invited to her friend Berenice Weinberg's for dinner the next evening, and, as was Nina's way, and, as if I had no social awareness, was duty bound to admonish me to dress nicely. *Ah,* I thought, *this told me that Nina was concerned with me acting properly and making a good impression on Berenice.* This was amusing, as it was I who was always concerned with Nina's wardrobe and behavior.

The next evening, we arrived at an elegant, beautifully gardened home in an upscale gated community. We were greeted at the door by Berenice, dressed in an understated jacket, shirt, necktie, and slacks. I was struck by this very attractive and sophisticated business-type woman with short dark auburn hair, piercing eyes, maybe late thirties or early forties, slender and athletic. Wow, I said to myself, Nina, don't ruin THIS relationship, this one looks like a winner. Berenice gave me a cordial hello and shook my hand while holding my arm, then she said, "Al, it is an honor to meet you. Nina speaks of you often. She tells me that you are the one person who has telepathic communication with her when you play, that you always know what she is feeling, and most importantly, that you are always there for her. That is so amazing."

After dinner, we sat with some brandy and coffee, talking for a while in the living room. I told her about meeting Nina for the first time, that playing with her was a mystical experience for me. Berenice said that she was really looking forward to hearing us together. She couldn't come to the North Sea Festival, but that she was going to come with us to Antibes. I was delighted to hear this. I could tell that she had deep feelings for Nina and hoped, even after just having met her, that this might evolve into a lasting relationship, if Nina could just let herself accept Berenice, and make peace with her obvious attraction toward another woman.

The next morning, we were off to the mountains and Nina's spa. It was a beautiful drive. I expected to find a typical spa offering massage, various types of beauty treatments, and baths, basically a women's luxury experience. I didn't see that at all. We were met by the director and a staff member, who welcomed us. I was introduced to the director, Dr. Hurwitz, who told the staff woman to take care of Nina, and off they went. The doctor then said to me, "Mr. Schackman, please, let's have a coffee, and I would like to have a chat with you concerning Nina."

I was beginning to get very suspicious of people inviting me to a coffee and a chat about Nina, but, "Lead the way," I said, and off we went to his office, which was, aside from his desk and a couple of file cabinets, a very comfortable living room with a panoramic view of Lake Geneva way off in the distance. The doctor ordered our coffee and related his concerns to me. "To be clear," he said, "this facility is not a spa. It is a cardio and neurosurgery center specializing in postsurgical rehabilitation. Miss Simone arrived here quite by chance. Drove up, came in, saw our pool, and announced herself to one of our therapists. Evidently, she thought she was at a spa, and while we do offer similar therapeutic treatments, this is a critical-care center. People are brought here after surgery and are patients, not spa-goers, but we were quite aware of Nina Simone's music and decided to show her every courtesy."

We paused for our coffee, but I knew that Dr. Hurwitz had more on his mind.

After a few moments, he continued. "That being said, we have welcomed Miss Simone's visits, and I have enjoyed having her company at lunch. In that time, I have observed her behavior as being quite erratic. Her mood swings and rambling dialogues regarding her misfortunes seem to consume her, as if she has nothing else to occupy her life."

"Dr. Hurwitz," I said, "you have just given me a most accurate and insightful analysis of Nina Simone. I have been at a loss in trying to help her. I'm not a professional counselor, just her trusted friend and colleague."

Dr. Hurwitz continued, "Of course, I sympathize with your position, Mr. Schackman. To stand by your friend while unable to help her cope with her dysfunction. I have seen this behavior in others, both clinically and personally. If I were to advise, I would strongly suggest that Miss Simone undertake a psychiatric program with a counselor who has a similar cultural background and can relate to Miss Simone on that level. I would also strongly suggest that she cannot receive that specialized help here in Europe. She would have to return to America."

"And therein," I replied, "lies the problem. Nina will not think of residing in America at this time and would be extremely angry if someone tried to persuade her toward that end. America is evil to Nina, and I cannot blame her for some of those feelings."

"Again, I completely understand your problem," he said,

"and as far as Miss Simone's visits, if it helps her and gives her a sense of security, she is welcome here, and we would not require any payment as we would consider her our friend."

"Dr. Hurwitz," I said, "this is completely gracious of you, and it's a relief to know that Nina can have an oasis here. "

"Yes," he said, "no palm trees, but we will try to be of help."

With that being said, we returned to the lounge where we found Nina engaged in conversation with the staff woman.

"Al," she said, "when we perform at the Montreux Jazz Festival, I want everyone from the spa to be my guest."

"But Nina," I said, "who will take care of the clients?"

"Al," she laughed, "don't make things so complicated," and with that, we bid our adieus and drove off on our way down the mountain.

Nina was quiet, drifted off into her own space for a while, and then she turned to me and sadly said, "You know, Al, I don't mind if you are playing along with me, but just so you know, I'm aware that it's not a spa, but when I'm there, I really feel taken care of and at peace inside myself. I'll take that wherever and whenever I can find it. If the world was as calm and accepting as that place back there, I think my life would be very happy."

Oh, Nina, I thought, *if only.*

The next morning, Saturday the 16th, Berenice was at the house and helped Nina pack for our upcoming concerts at North Sea and Antibes. She drove us to the airport, gave Nina a hug, kissed her on both cheeks as Europeans will, and said she would meet us in Antibes. During the flight, I mentioned again to Nina how impressed I was with Berenice, her affection for Nina, and how she seemed to care for Nina's well-being. Nina replied, a little coldly, that Berenice was asking too much of her. She didn't want to go there.

She continued, "Al, I really have feelings for Berenice, but don't want to be connected with a lesbian."

"I can understand your resistance," I said, "but if you look at it as a pure relationship between two people who care for each other, without putting labels or gender on it . . . ."

Nina's hackles rose. "Al, you're not listening! I'm not going there. You're pushing me. Now back off!"

"Fine, Nina, I just see something that . . ."

"AL!" she yelled.

Case closed.

We flew on in silence, Nina sipping on her champagne, looking out the window, and me wondering if Nina would ever be at peace within herself and hopefully come to a place where she might be able to consummate the meaningful ongoing relationship that she so desperately wanted.

It was maybe a couple of years later that Nina had given up her home in Switzerland and was living in Provence, France. I was there preparing for a concert with her, and we were reminiscing about Switzerland, when Nina suddenly came out and said, "Al, you were right about Berenice. I never got her out of my mind. She was a beautiful soul, and I acted like an idiot in rejecting her. I wish I could turn it around. What would you say to contacting her for me, seeing if we could repair the damage I caused? I tried phoning her, but the number was no longer in service."

"Nina," I said, "that sounds fantastic. Let's get through this concert, and I'll reach out to her."

I did try to find Berenice. True, her old phone was no longer working. She had resigned her position at the car company. They said they were very surprised by it and had no forwarding info for her. She sold her property and essentially dropped out. I located her family and contacted them. They were very hostile, sounded like they couldn't abide a lesbian, and hadn't had any contact with her for the past few years. Sadly, I conveyed all this to Nina. She was really upset and said it was a tough life lesson. "If that happiness door opens for you," she said, "y'better put your foot in it before it slams shut on ya. It don't stay open long."

Around 1984, while living in Nijmegen, Holland, our Dutch friend Gerrit Debruin, who was a trusted adviser to Nina, convinced her to have a medical checkup with a doctor friend of his. The doctor was also a psychiatrist and took Nina through a complete medical workup and talked extensively with her. At a later date, he met with Gerrit and me. He told us that Nina was manic-depressive, a term that was then used to describe a bipolar condition. Based on his interview with Nina and our descriptions of her violent and melancholy episodes, he felt that if she went untreated, she could possibly get to the point where she would have to be institutionalized for her own protection, as well as others.

He prescribed an antipsychotic drug, perphenazine, issued in the US under the name Trilafon, which he said could help control Nina's erratic and violent behavior, and could be taken in tablet form. He also cautioned that side effects from the drug, over the long term, could be significant and might include shuffling when walking, facial twitching, slurring of words, and a drop in her muscle coordination when at the piano. We were appalled at hearing this. He told us that these side effects might be mild, but that we needed to truly understand the alternative. Nina was a seriously, clinically troubled person.

We spoke to Nina about our session with the doctor. We had been given a supply of the medication, and she agreed to try it. I know that when we mentioned the possible alternative down the line, it scared her.

The medication was working, and I took responsibility for keeping the pills when we were on tour, carrying them in my guitar case in a 35mm film can with tape wound around it, saying, pills pills pills. There were times when Nina would ignore the medication, seemingly wanting to experience her manic state. She would say she wanted excitement. We just had to cope with the results of that behavior. Unfortunately, through the years, we definitely noticed the side effects that the doctor had described. Nonetheless, Nina was able to keep performing until her final tour in 2001.

EXCERPTS FROM LETTERS FROM NINA IN SWITZERLAND

April 4, 1977

Send me my money, Nigger! Toute de Suite. You h'yere? That's first. I need it. This sypcophantic lawyer here is TOO soft. If we get the loot from Paris, it'll be in "FOREVER" time. Meanwhile, I'm still surviving so SEND me my MONEY. Went on a rampage and spent too much at the Velvet Club the other nite, Took An —An "Entourage"! Yip-pee!! Had a ball!

Just saw "Hard Rain" with Bob Dylan on TV. My Brother (For True) – It scared me a bit. He sees something so deep and frightening that he's raining pain and ain't no body listening. They can't. I heard it. I saw it. God help me.

Listen nigger. Should I come back there for anything? Even the doctorate?

❀ ❀ ❀

August 2, 1977

. . . going into Hospital for checkup Monday A.M. What fun! Hospital looks like a plush Hotel. Swimming Poolsss. Fantastic view. Sleep cures. Anything you want. Luxury personified. The Arabs come there and actually use it for a Hotel . . . [Berenice] came through and is finally taking care of me! One less worry. Thank God. Thank [Berenice].

FROM HOLLAND

August 14, 1977

Al Dearest, Miss you Like Crazy...Been here one week (exactly today). Could not take one more day in house alone...[Berenice] started to get heavy AND deadly. Started to weaken under her, so "flew" out quick... If I'm not in Switzerland, I'm here.

Love you, miss you.

Nina.

THE NORTH SEA AND ANTIBES JAZZ FESTIVALS

IN 1977, there were a number of concerts during the year when Nina and I performed without the band. Two notable performances were at the North Sea in the Netherlands and the Antibes Festival in Juan Les Pins, France. For the North Sea concert, we had hired Michael Guilford, a fine American double bass, and tuba player who flew in from his home in Paris. His tuba added a distinctive color to our music.

NORTH SEA FESTIVAL

The Hague, Netherlands

Landing at Schiphol Airport in Amsterdam, we were met by Paul Acket, the founder of the North Sea Jazz Festival, who presented Nina with a bouquet of flowers. Nina was impressed and happy to have him personally greet her. This was the second year of the event, and it had immediately become the foremost jazz festival in Europe. I was thinking that this could be a big boost for Nina's popularity and reputation, if she could just maintain a cordial disposition.

The festival was an enormous affair, held that year in The Hague at the Congresgebouw, a complex similar to the Javits Center in New York, with dozens of jazz artists performing over a three-day period; Friday, Saturday, and Sunday, July 15-16-17, 1977.

Featured performers that year included Ella Fitzgerald, Dizzy Gillespie, Oscar Peterson, Nina Simone, and a fabulous French gypsy jazz band La Romanderie.

We had checked into the hotel and were sitting in the lounge having a drink, and I told Nina that our set was scheduled for Sunday afternoon at four p.m. Nina was upset at the timing.

"It's too damn early. I'll barely be awake," she said. "I'm a star and I should be appearing in the evening. Who in the hell put that schedule together?"

"Nina," I said, quickly thinking up something, "Sunday afternoon is the most popular time of the weekend in Holland. The hall is bound to be sold out. Tonight, we could have an early dinner and maybe afterward go over and catch some music."

"Maybe dinner," she said, "but I'm not goin' over to the festival until I have to play tomorrow. Sheesh, I should do the concert from my bed."

With that, Nina went to her suite for a nap while I met up with Michael. We walked over to the festival to check out the scene, survey the musical landscape, and establish our presence with friends and acquaintances. I was looking forward to making contact with La Romanderie and catching their set. I checked with the festival office, and they told me La Romanderie's set was scheduled for 6:45 p.m. that day in Bon Bini Zaal (hall), and they gave me a directory map for the events. *Yikes,* I thought, *some of the events are scheduled for 2:45 in the morning.* Then I remembered, we're in Holland in July, and so far north it's still light at midnight. People are boogying all night long.

I am deeply fascinated by all gypsy music, Nina as well.

Their fire is an underlying influence in my playing. When we were performing in Spain, we always tried to seek out the bistros where we could hear authentic flamenco music. The world of gypsy music is quite diverse, ranging from French to Hungarian to Spanish flamenco genres. My Dutch friend, Gerrit DeBruin, an aficionado of gypsy music, introduced me to their world, and strongly recommends listening to Hungarian cimbalom (tambal) music, especially the music of Alexandru Sura. He is phenomenal, jaw-dropping good. Also, of course, Django Reinhardt, the legendary French gypsy jazz guitarist. And in the world of flamenco, the traditional guitar of Sabicas, and the fiery contemporary guitar of Paco de Lucia will capture you. Masters all.

As it turned out, Nina wasn't up for joining Michael and me for dinner. She had seemed melancholy and pensive, saying she was lonely and looking forward to seeing her friend Berenice, who would join us in Antibes, our next scheduled performance after the North Sea Festival. I hoped she would not carry this particular mood onto the stage the next day. Of course, her moods always set the tone for her performances, and I was always prepared to expect the unexpected. One never knew where she might take her audience. That was her magic, but this unknown element kept me on my toes just before a performance.

Since Nina wasn't into joining us, I passed on dinner too. There was little time to get over to the hall to hear the gypsy band. I went to my room and picked up my little 1915 George Washburn parlor guitar. This tiny soulful little devil of a guitar, built from rosewood with a spruce face, would be just right if

I sat in to play somewhere that evening. It's the guitar that I used on Nina's recording of Bob Dylan's "The Ballad of Hollis Brown," her powerful driving version outdoes even Dylan's. It can be heard on the album *Nina Simone — The Phillips Years.* I'm also playing it on Joe William's recording of "Easy Rider," *on The Long Road to Freedom: an Anthology of Black Music,* produced by Harry Belafonte.

I got over to the festival just as La Romanderie began their set. Their sound was very much in the tradition of Django Reinhardt's music, and some members were actually related to him. Instead of incorporating a piano, they used an accordion, bringing a very warm sound to the group, which also included three guitars, bass, drums, and violin. After the set, I went back to meet them, and with one of them speaking English, we got along just great. They were very interested in hearing my little Washburn guitar and invited me out to where they were staying. Incredibly, where they were staying was out in back of the Convention Center, camped in a grassy area with their vehicles, six late-model Mercedes sedans and house trailers ringing their encampment with chairs spread out around a fire pit in the middle. They had their families with them, children running around and a clothesline with laundry hung between two of the trailers—a modern-day gypsy caravan. We sat down around the fire; a lady came out with some coffee for everyone. I took out my guitar, and they all wanted to hold it, like a baby. They passed it around with the guys strumming it a bit before passing it back to me. They couldn't believe that such a strong sound was coming out of this little old instrument.

The guitar players asked if I would like to play a tune together.

"Lead on," I said. They broke out their guitars and swung into a Django classic, "Minor Swing," which happened to be an old favorite of mine, and I joined right in. I was having a ball, and quite ready to pick up a Mercedes and a trailer somewhere and go touring with them. *Dream on, Alvin.* Needless to say, I had a ball, and after talking awhile, I told them about my playing with Nina. They said they would catch our set. Realizing they would be playing again, a one-hour set at 2:45 in the morning, I bid them goodnight, and off I went to check back into my Nina Simone world.

The next day, I had our soundcheck scheduled for eleven in the morning in order to give us enough time back at the hotel to relax, maybe have a bite to eat, and dress. Usually, Nina would leave the soundcheck to me, but she was awake, dressed, and insisted on coming.

"I'm going to find out who put this damned schedule together. Waking me up at an ungodly hour to do a show. And you, Al, as my music director, should have taken care of it. This is no way to treat a star, and I'm ready to tell Paul Acket. As the head of this festival, he should have this shit together."

Usually, if Nina wanted to attend the soundcheck, I would go over first and make sure the crew had finished setting up, and then I would call over to the hotel for Nina to come.

"No problem," I said, "your car is downstairs . . . let's go."

We arrived onstage, with the crew just finishing up, testing microphones and stage monitors. These guys had been working until four in the morning. They were good and didn't need to be harassed. Uh oh, Paul Acket was there, walked onto the stage and said, "Good morning, Nina, did you sleep well?"

Oh lord, I said to myself, *I didn't have time to warn him off.*

"How dare you treat me like a common club singer," she said.

How does she come up with these things?

"Nina," he said, "but . . ."

"Don't Nina me," she replied. "You ain't payin' me enough to get me outta bed this early. I oughta' charge you double."

I stepped in, and hoping to diffuse her, said, "Nina, come check out the piano, *it's a Bosendorfer.*" Bosendorfer is renowned to be the number one piano in the world, ahead of Steinway and Bechstein, and Nina loves playing on one. I got Nina's attention with this, and reluctantly, she allowed me to escort her to the piano, while turning to Paul Acket and saying, "At least you got something right!"

The soundcheck went well. Nina played up a storm on the piano, enjoyed Michael's tuba accompaniment, and felt better. It was good for her to work out like that, and she was in a better mood back at the hotel. I ordered a massage for her and some lunch, went to my room, and chilled out.

Then, it was approaching concert hour, and before I went ahead over to the hall, I stopped in at Nina's suite and we prepared the music list. She was upbeat, was dressing for the concert, and had just finished being on the phone with Berenice, who was all set to meet us in Antibes and had made her reservation at the historic Le 1932 Hotel and Spa where we would be staying.

"Al, I'm in the mood to do some Kurt Weill, Bertolt Brecht music," she said. "Let's include 'Alabama Song' from their opera, *Mahogany*, and Kurt Weill's 'Pirate Jenny,' from his *Threepenny Opera*. Also, don't forget Jacque Brel's 'Ne Me Quitte Pas,' 'I Loves You Porgy,' and of course, 'My Baby Just Cares for Me,' as an encore. You fill out the rest of the program and put it on the piano for me. See you over there."

After Nina's confrontation with Paul Acket that morning, I was really pleased to find her in such a jovial mood.

The concert went beautifully. Nina was at her best, and she had the audience in the palm of her hand, under her spell. Insisting on two encores, with Nina saying, "You're all like a bunch of spoiled babies wanting more candy, but momma loves you. I'll do one more, then it's goodnight." With that, she broke into "My Baby Just Cares for Me," and instead of singing the lyric, "my baby just cares for me," she sang, "my babies all care for me."

And to my relief, in her dressing room after the concert, Nina greeted Paul Acket with a big hug and said, "I hope you're happy now. I had a good time with my fans in spite of the abominable hour, and I expect you to invite me back next year. For more money of course."

Paul laughed, and I could tell that Nina had captured him as well.

"Of course, we'll have you back," he said. "You were sensational. It's a date."

And they did.

ANTIBES JAZZ FESTIVAL

Juan Les Pins, France

The day after our concert in Holland, we flew into Nice International Airport on the French Riviera. It was a beautiful sunny day, and there waiting for us was George Wein, the founder and impresario of the festival, holding a bouquet of flowers for Nina. Nina was excited and eager to meet up with Berenice, who had arrived earlier in the day.

I was looking forward to sitting in with Michel Legrand, the well-known film composer and songwriter who, unbeknownst to most, was also a fine jazz pianist. He had organized a late-night jam session at one of the venues, inviting a few musicians to play.

It was nice of George Wein to make it free of charge for those fans who wished to attend some fine midnight music. Michel Legrand is the Oscar-winning composer of the song "The Windmills of Your Mind," the theme from the 1968 original movie version of *The Thomas Crown Affair*. This song, to me, with its mysterious lyrics, stands out as a perfect example of how a piece of music can shape the opening of a suspense film. The jam session was a blast, with quite a few musicians showing up.

The next morning, I went down for breakfast, and there was Nina sitting with Berenice. Amazed, I said, "Nina, is that you? In the morning? In public, having breakfast?"

"Well, Al," she said, "Berenice is a good influence on me. We're going for a swim, and after lunch we're going shopping.

I need something casual to wear since the venue is outdoors tonight. This gig will be easy, we'll have some fun. You do the soundcheck and make up the set list. Just include our regular songs and be ready for whatever I throw in."

Ah, I thought, *this bodes well.* It's great when Nina is in a good mood and just wants to "wing it," but in a good way, committed to the music. She opens up, and we can improvise, invent and challenge each other. Maybe I should thank Berenice. I thought back to that time when we were on the flight to the North Sea Festival, Nina angrily coming at me when I brought up a possible relationship with Berenice.

"I'm not going to have a relationship with a lesbian," she yelled. And that was the end of it. I now wondered how long Berenice would allow herself to stay involved with Nina. Berenice was a class act. I knew she wouldn't let herself be a doormat, to be pushed away every time she got too close. But that was for another day. Right now, we were riding a nice wave, and it would settle on its own.

At this point, I need to say that this concert was a perfect example of Nina Simone at her best. Magical, at one with the audience, bringing them along through her myriad of emotions, joking with them, allowing them to share in her sadness as, like in her song "Don't Smoke in Bed" when she says, "I left a note on his pillow, with my old wedding ring, with these few goodbye words, how can I sing." She actually had left her husband, Andy, that way.

I had made out the set list and put it on the piano, but on this night, while Nina did perform some of the songs on the list, the evening evolved into a love-in with Nina singing whatever came through her in the moment. Here is the program as she performed it, which was broadcast on French radio and can be found in its entirety on YouTube: *Nina Simone-Festival de Jazz d'Antibes, 1977-07-19.* Her banter with the audience is memorable, and at times, she would immediately go into the next song right over the audience's applause.

1. Ne Me Quitte Pas
2. My Way
3. Plain Gold Ring
4. Please Read Me

Then she says, "Al, the lights. I can't see you." The lights are adjusted.

5. I Love to Love
6. Just say I love Him / (medley into)
7. Four Women
8. I Loves You porgy / (medley into)
9. A Single Woman

Talking with the audience, she says, "How do you like my attempt to be sexy?"

10. Let's Stick Together Blues

Nina leaves the piano, begins dancing with me playing the congas, and sings:

11. Be My Husband

Sits back down at the piano and goes into:

12. Alabama Song

Jokes with the audience, laughingly says, "If I say something about the microphones, they will say I'm being bitchy." Laughs.

Then goes into:

13. In Our Childhood's Bright Endeavor (spiritual)
14. In My Life / (medley into)
15. Let's Stick Together Blues
(*a reprieve, she motions for the audience to join in.)*

The evening ends.

Berenice was completely overwhelmed by Nina's performance. I think she was surprised at how dynamic Nina could be, since she had never before attended a Nina Simone concert, and this was a great one. She realized that Nina was a major star.

After the concert, I met up with my friend George Barrie, founder and CEO of Faberge, producer of the men's cologne, Brut. I had composed the musical score for the film *Book of Numbers,* starring Raymond St. Jacques, Phillip Michael Thomas, and Freda Payne, which was produced by his film company. George, a former musician and songwriter, was attending the festival and wanted to meet Nina. He invited us, together with Berenice, tomorrow, to his villa in the hills overlooking Antibes and the Mediterranean. We would all enjoy a nice afternoon together before going home, and George was a real down-to-earth kind of guy that Nina would appreciate meeting. Of course, she always enjoyed being in the company of the rich and famous.

The next afternoon, we arrived at George's villa, were welcomed and told that George was out by the pool, asked if we cared for something to drink, and Nina right up ordered a champagne. We were led out to the pool, a beautiful setting among cypress and palm trees, the scent of jasmine in the air. Idyllic. George was standing in the shallow end of the pool, talking with someone, and waved to us. Nina immediately put down her bag and began removing her clothes.

"Nina," I said. "Did you bring a bathing suit?"

"No, Al," she said. "I don't need a bathing suit. This is the French Riviera." With that, she took off the rest of her clothes, and ignoring a look of apprehension from me and Berenice, dove into the pool. Nina, being an expert swimmer, and at forty-four years of age, still in fine sleek condition, glided underwater and exploded out right behind this Troll-like redheaded man that George was talking with. She wrapped her arms around him and yelled, "Bonjour, I'm Nina Simone."

I could see that the man was shocked at being set upon by this Nubian creature coming out of the depths. George, kind of an old-guard conservative, was alarmed and quickly took hold of the situation. "Nina," he said. "I'm George Barrie, so good to meet you. I so enjoyed your performance last night. Let me introduce you to Patrick MacFarlane from Scotland, head of the North Sea Petroleum Exploration Company."

"Oh, an oil tycoon," Nina said. "Are you powerful?

I've always wanted an oil well. Then I wouldn't have to work so hard."

"Oh my," he said, in his very pronounced Scottish brogue. "I'm so sorry, Nina, but I am not that powerful."

George immediately stepped in and said, "Why don't we all go over to the terrace and have some refreshments." And to Nina he said, "I'll see to getting you a towel."

Nina eventually put her clothes back on, and Berenice lightened the atmosphere after Patrick, obviously attracted to her, asked about the kind of work she was in. She told us about her role in heading up GMC of Switzerland, and the problems involved in importing American cars, impressing everyone with her business acumen. I saw that while Nina was proud of being with Berenice, I could tell that she was also a little put off about not being the center of conversation. The light was not on her, as it usually was.

I asked George about his film, *Thieves,* which was released earlier that year, starring Marlo Thomas and Charles Grodin. I wondered about him having the music done by a team instead of a single composer. He said that it hadn't worked out badly, but he would like to hear the title song, which he composed with composer Sammy Cahn, done in a more personal style.

Nina, suddenly back on her game, said, "Well, I don't know the song, but you should have had Nina Simone sing it. She would have made it a hit."

George said, "Would you like to do it? I can send Al the orchestra tracks from the movie. And I have another song you might like, called 'Touch of Class,' from another of my movies."

Nina was excited, and I said, "Nina, we can drive up to

Montreux and record at Mountain Studios, just an hour's drive from your house. The studio is associated with the Montreux Jazz Festival, where you've performed, and they would love to have you do a session there."

George said, "Give me an address to forward the tapes, and I'll have them sent right out. I'll also have a performing rights agreement written up to protect your royalties."

Nina was quite impressed with George, and with this, it turned into a very successful get-together.

George was leaving on his jet the next day and asked us if we needed a ride.

Nina piped right up and said yes, it would be lovely if she and Berenice could be dropped off in Geneva.

"No problem," he said. I told him that I was headed back to New York from Heathrow in London and would much appreciate the ride.

The next morning on the jet, Nina was in her glory. Lounging in comfort while sipping on a mimosa. George had Nina Simone playing on the sound system, while she, putting on her magnetic charm, was totally capturing George. Give me your number, she said to him, "You can pick me up and fly me away to my next concert. We'll have a great time." George actually seemed eager to comply.

We dropped Nina and Berenice in Geneva, and on the way to Heathrow, George said how he was really looking forward to seeing Nina again, notwithstanding the nude swimming party.

I said, "George, in your position, I know you've handled many situations and personalities, and it's great that you've been with her in her up mood, but her downside is waaay way down and unpredictable. I would hope you could, or would, accept all the facets of who Nina is."

"Al," he said, "I much prefer to be around a Nina Simone than some of the dull encounters I've had to put up with. I'll send the music to you, and we'll take it from there."

We landed at Heathrow, George dropped me right near my departure gate, and we had a fond 'till next time.

Later, I did drive up to Montreux with Nina and the orchestra tapes that George sent. She recorded his song "Thieves," in English and did a very commendable French version. We also hired a well-known Swiss Dixieland band to back Nina singing George's fun song "Touch of Class," which turned out very well.

On my flight home, I thought of what George had said, that he would rather be in the presence of Nina than some dull encounters he had to put up with. I realized that this held true for me as well, both musically and personally. My life was very deeply involved, deeply connected in so many ways to Nina Simone, and I was glad.

RENEWING NINA'S PASSPORT

I WAS IN NEW YORK with Nina, preparing to embark on a concert tour throughout Spain that Raymond Gonzales had arranged. He was once again our agent and manager, after a really difficult period in which Nina was living alone, hand to mouth in Paris, occasionally playing in bars for pennies. No promoter would book her since she had been continuously failing to appear at concerts. After being assured by Nina that she would accept Raymond's direction in negotiating concert fees and his assurances that she would not be overworked, the band was brought back together, and the tour of Spain was contracted.

Everything in Nina's life had deteriorated. Looking at her in those days, one would immediately notice how raggedy her appearance was. Her clothes were just a mess. Not to say that she didn't know how to dress. Nina was very fashion conscious and loved to attend fashion shows. In 1990, when we were appearing in Paris at *The Olympia Theater* and staying at Le Grand Hotel, I had my daughter, Davi, sixteen, and my son, Kris, thirteen, with me. We were sitting in the lobby of the hotel after having lunch when Nina came out of the lift, saw us, and strolled over.

Looking at the kids, she said, "I'm off to a Nina Ricci fashion show. Would you like to go?"

"Sure," I said.

"Not you, Al, just the kids."

They jumped up. Nina took them by the hand and off they went in Nina's limo.

Not you, Al? Just the kids? Oh well, that's Nina. When they got back, Davi told me that it was fantastic. They were seated down front by the runway, and she couldn't believe the way everyone was fawning over their "Aunt" Nina.

So, that day in New York, I realized that if she was to begin touring again, something had to be done about her old wardrobe, and I suggested that we go shopping. At that point, she not only needed new clothes but had mentioned that her passport had just expired, so that needed to be attended to as well.

The passport office was in Rockefeller Center. On the way there, we browsed some women's shops on Fifth Avenue. We found a nice upscale shop, and Nina began trying on clothes. In and out of the dressing room she would go, choosing flashy dresses that were more appropriate for evening soirees than a daily wardrobe. She was having fun, and it was nice to see her excited, but we had to keep moving. I had to steer her away from the glitz.

"Nina," I said," you'll do much better shopping for fancy clothes when we're in Madrid or Barcelona. Let's try and keep it functional."

"Al, you're the one who took me shopping and now you're being a stick-in-the-mud."

But after going through a large assortment of more conventional attire, she picked two well-tailored suits, one in blue and one in red, that would be comfortable for traveling and general appearances, and a couple of nice blouses. Nina was delighted at getting "spruced up" as she put it, stayed in the blue outfit, and off we went for the passport.

It was late in the day, and I hoped we could get the passport without having to come back another time to pick it up, as we were flying out in two days. In we went. There was no one else in the waiting room, and the agent's window was closed. It looked like they were done for the day, so I rapped on the window to see if I could get someone's attention, and did I get some attention! A door opened, and a very large, matronly Black woman appeared, a gun strapped to her belt, and who was not pleased at the disturbance. I asked if it was possible for the lady to renew her passport that day.

The agent looked at Nina sitting across the room, pointed at her, and said in a gruff voice, "You're Nina Simone, aren't you?"

"Yes," Nina said.

"We know about you. You come with me," the agent said, still gruff. *"You stay here,"* she said to me as they disappeared behind the door to the back room.

I waited and waited, occasionally hearing someone shout, and at one point someone sarcastically laughed. *What was going on?* Then I heard Nina yell, and I was really worried. I couldn't understand anything going on back there. *Was Nina in trouble? Was she wanted for something I didn't know about?* Almost an hour passed, and then the door opened. Nina came out, followed by the agent, and two more, also very large and formidable, Black ladies in uniform. They were laughing, hugged Nina, and said, "If you ever need something, you come and see us, you hear?"

Nina looked at me and said, "We're done. Let's go."

Outside, I said, "Nina, what the hell just went on in there?"

"Al," she said, "those girls were like my sisters, and they carried guns. They even let me hold one. How cool is that? We just started telling stories and had us a great old time."

"That's just fine, Nina, but all that yelling really got me worried. Knowing you, I thought you were being arrested. Oh, and by the way, what about your passport? Remember? That's why we came here."

"Oh sure," she said. "Here it is, take a look."

I took the passport, looked at the info page and said, "Good, that's a relief."

"No, Al, take a good look."

I looked again, and then I saw it. "Oh my god, c'mon," I said. Unbelievable. Nina and I were the same age, but I was looking at the passport, and there on the birthdate line, it read, Birthdate: February 21, 1943. It should have read, Birthdate: February 21, 1933.

"Yeah, Al, the agents just made me ten years younger." She looked at me and let go with one of her mischievous little giggles as we walked up Fifth Avenue to Central Park and to Rumplemayer's for an ice cream soda. All in all, a very sweet and memorable day with Sister Nina.

JAMES BALDWIN . . . JIMMIE

FAMED AUTHOR, novelist, essayist, and civil rights champion Jimmie Baldwin's essay in 1963, *The Fire Next Time,* was a warning to white America of the consequences that would befall them if the oppression of Blacks continued. He is imploring people to speak up, and ends his essay with these words:

> *If we—and now I mean the relatively conscious whites and the relatively conscious blacks, who must, like lovers, insist on, or create, the consciousness of the others—do not falter in our duty now, we may be able, handful that we are, to end the racial nightmare, and achieve our country, and change the history of the world. If we do not now dare everything, the fulfillment of that prophecy, recreated from the Bible in song by a slave, is upon us. God gave Noah the rainbow sign, no more water, the fire next time!*

I believe that Jimmie would think that the fire IS now upon us.

What jumps out for me in remembering Jimmie is his huge bright eyes and beaming smile, letting me know I was secure inside our friendship. His only requirement being honesty. While Jimmie was slight of stature, almost frail, he could wither someone with a look that they would think came out of a fire-eating dragon. He was truly a warrior. As a friend, being in his company was like riding a zephyr. "Al! What do you think about that . . . , or, what did you experience when . . . , or, tell me, did you hear what was said about . . . ?" Endless rapid-fire engagement, asking you to participate in processing whatever he was thinking or working out in the moment, and he's not only engaged you, but he's also touched you, he's captured you . . . with his mind.

I first met Jimmie at the Selma to Montgomery March. In the years that followed, Jimmie would at times appear in the audience at a Nina show, and, like an answer to a prayer, jump onstage if Nina was creating a difficult situation. He would grab a stool and just sit by the piano and smile at her. One time, in Paris, he actually represented her in negotiating with a concert promoter, a tough Russian, who was going to hold back on paying her performance fee. The promoter thought, mistakenly in this instance, that it was her late arrival that was responsible for most of the audience leaving and demanding a refund on their tickets. Yes, she was late, but it was the promoter's crew that messed up by forgetting to dispatch the limo to bring her back from the hotel.

(See the following chapter.)

THE POWER OF NINA SIMONE: THE ART OF KIDNAPPING A ROLLS-ROYCE WITH JAMES BALDWIN

It was rare, but for once, Nina was not responsible for the events that led up to this Rolls caper. Jackie Lombard was a concert promoter in Paris, backed by a Russian so-called "financier." To say that she and Nina didn't see eye to eye on almost everything regarding Nina's services is a gross understatement. They just didn't like each other. This held true as well in Jackie's dealings with our manager and agent, Raymond Gonzalez. As an example, Jackie booked a concert for us at the Palais des Congres, a large venue seating close to 4,000 people. The hall had a movable wall halfway down that could be closed to accommodate a smaller capacity. Nina learned that Madame Lombard was going to close the wall, and thus she refused to perform if the hall wasn't completely open.

"Who does that bitch think she is?" Nina said. "I am Nina Fucking Simone, the High Priestess of Soul, and my performance will be standing room only." Raymond argued about it with Jackie, her point being that it wouldn't look good for the press to report that the house was only half full. Of course Nina prevailed, and Jackie was forced to relent. I did the sound check the afternoon of the concert, which Nina attended, something rare for her. I looked out at the hall, and indeed it was vast.

I said to Nina, "Sure is a big place."

She laughed and said, "Al, this is Paris, and my people will pack the place." The night of the concert arrived, the announcer introduced us and out we went to rousing applause from a full house and then some.

❈ ❈ ❈

Now to the details of the Rolls-Royce caper . . . Jackie booked Nina into the Théâtre des Champs-Élysées for two performances on the same day. For some reason, Raymond Gonzalez was not involved in negotiating this booking. The matinee went very well and was to be followed by an early evening concert, with a break in between. Rather than rest in her dressing room, Nina decided to return to her hotel, which was only a couple of blocks away, where she would be more comfortable. When it was time to return to the theatre, a car would be waiting out front. The car was a Rolls-Royce Silver Spur, which the Russian money man had made available for Nina's use during her stay in Paris and was driven by a very nice young nondescript chauffeur named Arnaud.

Of course, something went wrong. It was time for the evening performance, the house was filled, the audience was restless, and no Nina. Back at the hotel, the phone had been blocked in her room with a "do not disturb" on it, and the people in Jackie's crew thought that someone else was in charge of seeing that Nina was on hand.

I was sitting at a café next to the theatre with James Baldwin. He was one of the few people in her life whom she totally trusted. We thought we'd best be getting back to the theatre, thinking that Nina was in her dressing room, but instead found everyone backstage freaking out. They couldn't contact Nina, and the audience was stomping. Jimmie and I ran back to the hotel and roused Nina. She dressed, we jumped in the Rolls, and back we went.

At least half the audience had left, but we went on with the performance and afterward returned to the hotel with Jimmie. According to the contract, Nina was to receive payment that night. As the three of us were having dinner in the hotel restaurant, Jackie Lombard came in and announced that the Russian was refusing to pay because Nina broke the contract by not performing as arranged.

Thank the heavens for Jimmie being with us to try to dampen the explosion, because all hell broke loose. Nina grabbed a dinner knife to attack Jackie, but Jimmie held her back while I took Jackie out to the lounge to try to find out what the deal was. Jimmie got Nina back up to her suite, telling her that we would straighten everything out. He came back down into the lounge where the huge Russian "whatever-he-was" declared that Nina would not see any payment. *Oh boy, a real classic Nina Simone mess.*

Jimmie took me aside and said, "Al, you cover Nina. See that she doesn't come down here, and I will negotiate with the Russian."

Up I went to Nina, and she was surprisingly calm.

"Al, he is going to pay up one way or another."

"What do you mean?" I said. "Jimmie is negotiating with Jackie Lombard and the Russian. Let him do his thing."

"That's all very well and good, Al, but here's what we're going to do."

Nina calm? Hmm . . . I knew she had something up her

sleeve and that it couldn't bode well. We went downstairs and out the front, with Nina leading the way. The Russian's Rolls was parked at the curb with Arnaud, the driver, behind the wheel. Nina said, "Al, get in, we're going for a drive." I helped Nina in; she scrunched over behind Arnaud, and I told Nina that I had to let Jimmie know privately that we were taking the Russian's Rolls, going for a drive, and they could reach us on the car phone. I did that and then went back out and jumped in the Rolls.

Nina said, "Arnaud, start driving."

He said, "Where to, Madame Simone? I'm supposed to be waiting for the boss."

Nina said, "Oh, he told me it was fine to use the car for whatever I needed. We'll just go for a drive."

We started off. Arnaud, unhappy, said, "Please, Madame Simone, I have a family. I will lose my job."

Nina unleashed her plan. "Arnaud, right now, what is the fastest way to the Swiss border?"

"But, Madame Simone . . ."

"No buts, Arnaud, you now belong to me," and she poked him hard in the back of the head.

"Okay, okay. It's the A6, and it takes at least three to four hours."

"Get on it now, Arnaud. You're a good boy. Put some Nina Simone music on."

Off we went, with decanters of brandy, vodka, and champagne resting in the little bar.

Nina was in her glory, having the time of her life, whispering to me, "Remember, Al, we have friends in Geneva who will help us sell the Rolls on the fringe market without any paperwork, and still make far more than we would have made with the concert, if I should decide to not keep it, as it befits my stature."

"But Nina . . ."

"Al, don't chicken out on me."

"But Nina . . . when we get to the border, the customs people will want to see the car's paperwork, and what about Arnaud? He's bound to say something."

"Not if I pay him a few thousand to shut up. As for the border people, I'm Nina Fucking Simone, remember?"

Ohhkaaayy, I thought, *a fine waltz you got us into this time, Nina.* We had been on the road for about an hour when the car phone suddenly rang. I picked it up, and it was Jimmie.

"Al, where are you? They agree to pay tonight's fee if we will agree to perform two concerts, future dates and fees to be discussed. I told them Nina would be happy to do the dates, half the fees up front, and they agreed. Please, you have to come back with the Rolls."

I turned to Nina, told her that Jimmie settled with the Russian, and she yelled, "You men are all weak. You take the fun right out of everything."

I said to Arnaud, "Back to Paris," and so back we went with a now sullen Nina drinking champagne and consoling herself over losing out on acquiring a Rolls-Royce Silver Spur.

Jimmie and the Russian were waiting for us. The Russian, relieved to have his car back in one piece, said to Nina in a heavy Russian accent, "Madam, you are very lucky to have such a formidable protovnik (opponent) to negotiate for you."

Nina replied, "And YOU are very lucky I didn't keep your

car AND your very cute driver. AND my concerts will cost you a lot more than these two concerts did."

Well, Nina later declared to Raymond Gonzalez, her longtime agent and loyal friend, that she would no longer perform for less than $30,000 per concert, unheard of for a jazz artist, even more than Miles Davis was getting. Raymond, although reluctant to attempt it, did indeed successfully negotiate Nina's $30,000 fees.

And thank you, James Baldwin, dear friend and international negotiator, for saving the day.

NINA SIMONE MEETS ZEN MEDITATION

IN 1974, Nina had recently purchased a poolside condo apartment on Franklin Avenue in Hollywood. She was flying back and forth from Europe and seemed unsettled, and kind of bored with herself. We had recently completed a concert tour of Japan, Australia, and New Zealand, and she returned to her condo. I was living at my farm in Massachusetts, and while I was on the phone with her one day, she said she was needing something to do as she was going stir crazy. From speaking with her, I definitely felt that she was in an unstable frame of mind, so I mentioned the possibility of her taking up Zen meditation. I had some close friends in Santa Monica, members of the Arica School, who held a very relaxed Zen meditation circle that met twice a week. I was sure they would welcome her and said I would set it up, if Nina were at all interested, and she said she would love to try it. I phoned my friend, Susan Branaman, who said Nina would be welcome, and she would be glad to drive Nina to and from the meeting. I phoned Nina and said it was on.

Nina said, "Al, okay, but don't be putting me in the middle of a bunch of hippies and weirdos."

I said, "Nina, this is a group of very wealthy people. Susan, whose family is the Mack Truck Manufacturing Company, will be driving you. She's a wonderful person, really an angel come to earth, and you'll love being with her."

"Well," Nina said, "I could use some angels in my life right now. All the record companies are trying to steal my money."

"No fear," I said. "These people have plenty of their own money and don't need yours."

"Fine," she said. "I always feel better when I'm around people with money."

I phoned Susan with Nina's number, asked her to arrange the meeting, and told her that Nina could be temperamental.

Susan laughed and said, "Al, I've dealt with loads of temperamental. We'll be fine."

This is how Susan related the episode to me later: "Al, I phoned Nina, and she was very nice. We arranged for me to pick her up, and she was surprised that I was driving a Toyota and not a Mercedes, or a Mack truck. I got that you told her about my family, so I told her I had problems with them. She told me she had problems with her own family, and that she understood. We had a nice drive over to the facility, parked, and headed in.

"I had told her to dress comfortably since we would be sitting on cushions, and she arrived dressed very nicely. She was carrying a very large shoulder bag, and I told her she wouldn't need it in there, but she said she always carried it with her. In the entrance, we took off our shoes, then went into the meditation hall, a very calming room with light green walls and a plush dark green carpet. I introduced Nina to everyone, and they were delighted to meet "THE" Nina Simone.

"We picked up a cushion to sit on, formed a circle, and I sat Nina beside me. She put her bag down between us. We each put our hands together, bowing slightly while chanting a traditional 'OM.' We came back up, Nina looked around, put her hand inside her bag, and came back out with a .38 caliber revolver and put it down by her side. I immediately put the gun back into her bag, got Nina up, and ushered her out to the hallway.

"I calmly told her that a gun wasn't needed in Zen meditation. She said, 'Zen samurais used to carry swords, but she carried a gun because she didn't know what she would run into.' She wouldn't leave the bag in the office, so that was the end of that.

"I drove her home while she talked about the music business in Los Angeles being shady and run by the Mafia. I dropped her off at her condo. She thanked me and said she had a nice time meeting everyone but didn't like the sound of their OM chantings. 'They were all out of tune.'"

MR. AL GOES TO HOLLYWOOD

IT WAS PRETTY COLD and snowy, as usual, that winter of 1980 in the pristine Berkshire highlands of Massachusetts. I was sitting in the control room of my recording studio, in the barn at my farm, when my friend, Richard Wechsler, called from warm and sunny Hollywood. He was the associate producer of *Palmerstown,* a new TV series written and co-produced by Alex Haley, the author of *Roots,* and TV sitcom icon Norman Lear.

Richard said, "The two-hour premiere is currently in production and is at a point where music is being considered. The series is based on Alex Haley's childhood in Henning, Tennessee, in the early 1930s, and might be right up your alley for composing the score. The story centers around ten-year-old Alex, (Booker T. in the film), and his best friend, David, who is white. If you have a piece of music that you think might be appropriate for this story, send it out to me, and I will see that Alex gives it a listen."

I did have a guitar piece, inspired by the pastoral hills of the Berkshires. I thought this piece might capture the rural spirit they were looking for. I sent it out to Richard and shortly heard back from him saying that Alex learned that I played with Nina Simone, loved my music, and thought that the piece would actually be perfect for the opening theme in the main titles. He invited me out to LA to talk with him about composing music for the series.

Working in the film industry? In the belly of the Hollywood beast? I had studied orchestration at Columbia University for only one year on the G.I. bill after I got out of the army. *Could I do it? Should I do it?* It would be a dramatic change in my life, both musically and personally. It would mean moving to Los Angeles, the fast track, writing for episodic television complete with the intensity and stress of producing a finished musical score every week, ready for dubbing on the sound stage with no room for correcting any discrepancies. *Was I up to this challenge?* I would soon find out. A ticket was arranged and waiting for me at Hartford International Airport, a two-hour drive from my farm.

I flew into LAX and was met by my old friend Bruce Langhorne, who insisted I stay with him at his house in Venice while I negotiated the Hollywood minefields. Bruce was by then an accomplished film composer, having worked on many major projects, including films produced by Peter Fonda. With his experience in the industry, his advice was going to be of great help. He was also going to put me in touch with his agent, saying it was essential for me to have representation in negotiations with the film company, if it was decided that I was their choice.

"Don't try and negotiate on your own," he said. "The sharks will have you for lunch and dinner."

The next day, I met up with Richard Wechsler, who arranged for me to meet Alex Haley, and then talk with the producer, Ron Rubin, regarding the production details and my participation in the film. Essentially, it would be up to Ron to give me the job. Before meeting with Ron, I was led into Alex's office and was greeted warmly by Alex and his friend and business partner,

George Sims. They were both impressed with my music and thought it had the right feel for the characters and the period in which the film was set.

They were highly interested in my relationship with Nina Simone. *I knew that would come up.* They wanted to know how I handled working with her, given her temperamental nature. Of course, they had heard all the stories about her, but were sincere in wanting to hear about "the real stuff" coming from my close ties to Nina. We wound up having a spirited time talking over coffee, with Alex welcoming me to the fold and saying that his door was always open to me. *Was I already hired?* I still had to meet with Ron Rubin.

Into Ron's office we went. He jumped up from his desk and enthusiastically stuck out his hand. We sat down, and he immediately went into describing his own ideas about the music. I listened, agreed with some of his ideas, and contributed my own take. He thought maybe a banjo would be appropriate. *Oh no,* I thought to myself, *not that!* I learned later that his son took banjo lessons.

I replied that, based on what I had been told, the series already had a rural homespun feel, so the music didn't need to accentuate the period any further. As an example, I said it would be similar to the music I sent for their approval, which I felt was rural enough. I said that I would need to see some of the rushes that had been shot to get a better idea of the general character. Ron said that it would be possible and concluded our meeting without giving me a commitment.

Hmm, I thought, *am I in no-man's land or what?* Well, maybe that's the way they work out here, but with the premiere just about done, there wouldn't be much wiggle room in the time needed to compose and produce the entire score. Not much time at all.

Am I in, or not? I asked Richard about it, and he understood the problem. "I'll try and move this along," he said. "To my knowledge they haven't approached anyone else as yet. Music has just been forgotten about until it suddenly came up in a production meeting, and that's when I called you. Just hold tight, and we'll get it sorted out."

I returned to Bruce's house and related the scenario at the meeting. Bruce was not at all surprised. "Sometimes," he said, "a decision won't come down until it goes through an executive group meeting, no one wanting to accept sole responsibility for the music in the event the show is reviewed negatively. At other times, like in this case, it's the producer's sole decision, and if he is not really sure about what genre of music is appropriate for the movie, it gets ignored until the eleventh hour. Rest assured, though, at this point in the production a decision ultimately has to be made. Don't let the "banjo" remark bother you. He's just trying to sound musical. If I'm hired for a project, it's because they want what I can bring to the movie. With some movies, the music really has to carry the action. When scenes lack their own power, it's essential that they can ride on the music. You have to stand your ground if you find yourself in the middle of confusion over how they might want you to play a scene. This can happen a lot, especially in a mediocre production. Keep an open ear but remember that you are the music boss. They hired you for your expertise."

Richard phoned the next morning and said that we had a

two o'clock meeting with Ron and would get it all resolved. We met up at the studio and sat down with Ron, who talked around things for a bit, suddenly stood up, banged his fists on the desk, and said, "You're our composer. You've got the job. We need the score for dubbing in two weeks. You'd better get to work." And that was it.

Well, Al, *you wanted it, now you've got it. BUT . . . how about a contract, my fee, getting with the director to spot the film for music cues? Entries and exits, all that critical stuff?* Then I would need a locked video work tape, which would mean no more editing. It would have a running time code of the final edit, so I could start timing the scenes. This would all be before I even put down the first note. *Two weeks?* Oh boy, welcome to Hollywood.

With my contract successfully worked out, I got down to the business of creating my music score. I was introduced to the director, Peter Levin, and we sat down together with a copy of the film and decided where music would enter and exit the scenes that we chose for underscoring. I came away with my book of music cues for each scene and was ready to compose. My immediate objective was to create the themes that would play under the main titles and end credits. These would be given to a large orchestra. For the main titles, I used an arrangement of my Berkshire Suite that Alex Haley had said he liked.

The volume of music to write was huge, given the deadline I was locked into. I spoke about my time constraints with Johnny Mandel, an old New York friend, who was the composer for the hit TV series, *Mash*, and the composer of the classic "The Shadow of Your Smile." He said that he often used someone to orchestrate his themes when he had that problem, and put me in touch with his orchestrator. It worked out well as it gave me the freedom I needed to compose.

Johnny also gave me the name of his music contractor, who would hire the orchestra and oversee the musicians during the recording sessions. Our film company booked Evergreen Studios in North Hollywood, one of the top sound stages, and I arrived with my music editor, Johnny Mick, who would oversee the timings of the music cues, making sure that they were synchronized with each scene as we recorded to the film being shown on a movie screen. I had to ignore the VIP audience sitting on a sofa at the control room window. Alex Haley was sitting there with George Sims, producer Norman Lear, and their friends. And this, my first major film scoring gig.

The session was an eye-opener for me. *Palmerstown* is the story of two families, one white and one black, in the 1930s segregated South. During a break in the session, Alex took me aside and told me how much he was liking my score, but quietly said in my ear, "Al, this orchestra is all white." *Oh no,* I thought. I had relied on Johnny's contractor to hire the musicians, knowing that Johnny had been an arranger for the Count Basie Orchestra. Johnny was white, a New York Jew, and I knew he was not racist. I had personally requested that Jerome Richardson, a great saxophonist and flutist friend, also from New York and who was Black, be on the session. I looked out at this forty-piece orchestra and, sure enough, they were all white except for Jerome and a cellist. Oh, and there was only one woman, the harpist, who was the wife of the studio manager. I had never even considered that racism could rear its ugly head on this project. I went up to the contractor after the session and asked about his choice of musicians, and he floored me with his comeback. "Black musicians are okay for R&B and black-themed films," he said, "but they're not ready for this level of work."

"WHAT?" I yelled. "You have got to be kidding me." I was totally blown away. This was Johnny Mandel's contractor. This was 1980, and I was at a loss for words. Well, there was one thing I could do, and I did it right there on the spot. I fired the contractor and the orchestra. What an introduction to Hollywood!

I got together with Jerome, who really opened my eyes to the industry machinery, and he was sorry I had to run into this on my first shot out of the starting gate. He told me that he recorded a lot at Group IV Studios, run by old New York guys, and I would feel really comfortable recording there. He also put me in touch with Billy Byers, a fine New York trombonist with whom I had played sessions back East. *Yeah, I was definitely liking the idea of a New York frame of mind.* Billy was now running a music copying service and contracting musicians for sessions, as well as staying busy as an arranger and orchestrator. "Okay," I said, and made some calls. The result was a wonderful experience, with the orchestra made up of a rainbow of musicians, including two Vietnamese ladies on cello. I made sure that Alex was at the session.

He said to me, "Brother Al, I knew you would respond to the situation. I'm proud of you. It had to be a difficult career move considering the politics involved out here. People talk. I've run into it myself."

"Alex," I said, "I hope they talk up a storm because, to use an old movie cliche, "Frankly, Scarlet, I don't give a damn." Thus began my Hollywood adventure.

My typical schedule went something like this. *Sunday:* Write melodic sketches that I felt were appropriate for each scene. *Monday:* Begin writing music, lay out my music cue book, two books if I were working on two separate projects at the same time. *Tuesday:* Continue writing, shaping my themes and music cues to match the timing of the scenes. *Wednesday:* Into the recording studio, usually late afternoon or early evening, thankfully having free rein at Bruce Langhorne's Blue Dolphin studios where my sessions could run all night. *Thursday:* finish recording, mix all the tracks, and get them over to the Transfer Lab where my 1/4" music tape would be transferred onto a magnetic stripe set into a 35mm film reel for our sound engineer to work with. *Friday:* the dubbing stage. All the elements are mixed together to form the completed film, and if everything went well on Friday? *Saturday:* I would take the day off.

During breaks in the *Palmerstown* series, I picked up other work, such as the CBS *Afternoon Playhouse* starring Tyne Daly. I was beginning to gain some industry recognition, but it was starting to take its toll and to affect my sense of well-being. My creative juices were being pushed to a point where I was beginning to question my musical values, not to mention all-night sessions with questionable "pick-me-ups." Sure, I was keeping my hand in on my playing chops, performing the guitar, piano, and bass parts in my arrangements, but I wasn't really *playing.* Not what I would call PLAYING. I was losing my spirit and realized that I had worked myself into a rut, trapped myself, and had to get out. Hollywood was a real test of my abilities, and I had nothing more to prove. While the paydays were great, I knew I had to make a change.

Here was my plan. Maybe I could get away with working from the studio in my barn back home, without Hollywood getting wind of it. I arranged for a new telephone that would have a Los Angeles number, but would ring back home in my barn. No one would have to know I wasn't in Hollywood. I would contract an assignment, record the score, and fly out to LA for the final mixing of the film. *Hmm. Could that work? Would that solve the problem, or would I just be fooling myself? What if there was a production meeting where I was required to attend?* Only time would tell.

I knew one thing for certain, without a doubt, I had to get back to playing with Nina, and she had to get back to some serious playing as well. Her time had not been well spent recently. She had been in Paris where she was working in a small bar for low money and tips, as promoters were afraid to book her because of her explosive temperament. Nina had decided she wanted to do cameo appearances in movies, and someone secured a role for her in a sci-fi film playing the part of an alien monster. Alex Haley happened to be visiting the film set, was introduced to her, and afterward said to me, "Brother Al, I met your friend Nina the other day and I have to tell you, she smelled of the grape." In other words, she was drunk. This was really disconcerting. I tried to reach Nina and learned that she was only on the movie set for one day, and they had no idea where she had gone.

I told Alex how I was having trouble managing the Hollywood scene and, surprisingly, he told me one of the reasons he was away on speaking engagements so much was that the movie world wasn't his "cup of tea," as he put it. He felt that he lost touch with his inner voice when he was immersed in the business of Hollywood. Alex really helped clarify the feelings I had been wrestling with, and not long after, I wound up saying goodbye to the LA scene and moved back to Massachusetts.

About a month after I was back, I was in my studio, and the phone rang. It was Nina's agent, Raymond Gonzales, phoning from Paris. Our percussionist, Leopoldo Fleming, was with him. He said that Nina was in Paris, promised to behave, wanted to go on tour again, and would allow Raymond to handle all the business if I would put the band back together. "Promised to behave?" I said to myself. *We'll see.* I hoped that everything could work out well and would put Nina back on her feet. "Okay, Raymond," I said, "I'm in, book us a tour." And he did.

It turned into a huge and very well-received tour of Spain. We played Bilbao, Oviedo, Marbella, Malaga, Murcia, Alicante, Barcelona, Madrid and Valencia in the Plaza de Toros, where in the dark of night we had to walk over a narrow footbridge above a bunch of fighting bulls bellowing in their corral down below, in order to get to the stage and 7,000 Nina fans, many holding votive candles in tribute. The music was pure Nina. She was terrific, gracious, enjoying herself, and how wonderful it was to be with her again in this environment.

JAPAN

WHILE TRAVELING the world performing, I was very fortunate to be able to explore and experience diverse cultures. The reason I had my own time was that Nina Simone had very demanding rules in regard to our concert tours, which included a travel day, followed by a rest day, the concert day, a rest day, and then a travel day. This meant one concert in five days, whereas most tours would book three to four concerts a week. Not that lucrative for our band members, as we counted on these tours to fill our coffers. Raymond Gonzales, our manager, expressed to Nina that with so few concerts, she didn't come away with as much as she could. Nina's reply was, "So, charge more money, but I'm NOT going to have you work me like a dog!!" Thus, I had plenty of free time in cities across the world, giving me opportunities to explore.

NARA AND KYOTO

During the concert tour to Japan, I took the opportunity during a break in our schedule to visit Nara, the ancient capital of Japan. The city has significant temples and artwork dating to the eighth century, and I was eager to explore these sites after reading and studying about them back home. In Nara Park, I wanted to find the site of the Tōdai-ji temple's huge forty-five-foot-high bronze buddha, which was on display in its own hand-hewn wooden hall. Also, in the park was the Shinto shrine Kasugai Taisha, which dated back to 768 A.D.

I was going to be staying in Kyoto at a traditional Japanese inn, with just a short local train ride to Nara. The Tokyo production company who had booked our tour made the arrangements for my trip and put me on the bullet train, explaining beforehand with a little trepidation, that I would be staying with very conservative hosts at the Inn, and I should be respectful of their manners and mannerisms. I told them not to worry. I would not embarrass them.

The ride down to Kyoto was beautiful, passing Mount Fuji, farm after farm, meticulously groomed and most with little solar hot water units on the roofs of their houses. This was way before they were popular in the States.

Arriving at the Kyoto main train station, I found a taxi, gave the driver the address that had been written out for me, and after a short drive through the town center, arrived at what looked like a very old Swiss country inn made of thick timbers. Not at all what I expected. It was an antique. I rapped on a heavy wrought iron knocker, the door opened, and an older man in a business suit and bow tie answered the door and greeted me.

"Ah, Shakuman San," (San used as a formal measure of respect), "hajimemashita," (so pleased to meet you)." Shakuman was as close as he could come to pronouncing my name.

"Mr. Tanaka San," Mr. and Mrs. Tanaka were the names I had been given, "hajimemashita," I said, and in I went with my bag to a vestibule where I hung up my jacket, took off my shoes, and was given a pair of slippers. A lady appeared, his wife, who was dressed in a plain modern-day blouse and skirt. "Hajimemashita, Mrs. Tanaka San," I said to her and bowed. She took in her breath, and half covering her mouth, said something to her husband that I hoped was recognizing my formal politeness. I realized right then, as I had been warned, that English was not spoken, and I might be the first foreigner to ever stay there. The lady started up the stairs, pointed to my bag, and bade me to follow her to my room.

It was a tatami room, bright and lovely, with a vase of flowers on a small low table, a bathroom, and notably, the floor covered with traditional straw tatami mats. I did not see a bed but was sure that these details would be taken care of and didn't ask. Mrs. Tanaka pointed to a number on her wristwatch while talking and pointing downstairs. I said, "Hai," (yes), and bowed as she left the room. I would be expected with the other guests downstairs for social tea before dinner.

Two couples arrived in the "social room," bowed to the Shinto shrine at the far end of the room, and after the customary salutations, everyone took seats on cushioned benches along each wall, and conversation started up. I sat there politely, until one of the guests turned to me and said in English, "Please excuse, but we are having curious talking about you coming here. Very interesting. Never for Mr. and Mrs. Tanaka before you. I am Mr. Amato, professor in history at National University in Yokohama." At that, everyone laughed and began throwing questions at me through Mr. Amato. A girl entered in a kimono, carrying a tray with tea, served, bowed, and left.

We all relaxed and had a fine time, me asking questions as well, through Mr. Amato.

I mentioned that I would be performing a concert with Nina at Mr. Amato's university soon, and he said he would be sure to attend. They were in awe of my being a musician. Artists in Japan were held in the highest esteem, and some were even designated National Treasures, financially supported by the government. The girl returned in the doorway and announced dinner. Mr. and Mrs. Tanaka led the way to the dining room, a tatami room where we sat on cushions with our feet down in a well and a table in the middle. The food was excellent. I surprised everyone with my use of chopsticks and knowledge of the various dishes, naming them in Japanese and English.

My visit was wonderful and heartwarming. I explored Nara and saw the great buddha and the shrines. When it was time for me to leave, I felt my host's sincerity in their pleasure at having me and wishing me a formal "seishikina sayonara, (a sad farewell)." Mrs. Tanaka gave me a beautifully wrapped gift. On the train, I opened it and found a hand-embroidered silk handkerchief, perhaps to use on my now-damp eyes.

BASEBALL

I arrived back at Tokyo Station and found "Spike" waiting for me. "Hi, man, how you doing?" he said in English, being very cool. No "Konnichiwa," the formal greeting, for this modern-day hip dude wearing a motorcycle jacket, jeans, boots, and sporting aviator sunglasses.

He and his young buddies, who were working for Tats Nagashima's production company, were like all the young urbans who I met worldwide. So many were speaking English, and slang English at that, examples of a New World culture on this shrinking planet. Spike took my bag, and I followed him out to his car, and off we went to the hotel. On the way, he brought up a previous conversation we had about baseball and how avid his guys were about the industrial baseball league they were in. I mentioned that I had played first base on my high school team, and so now they were hoping I would be the secret weapon in their upcoming game against a tough team.

"Sure," I said, "it would be an honor, but I don't want to take away someone else's position."

"No," he said, "we switch around anyway, and it would be our honor."

I attended their next practice, and these guys played hardball, were good, and were impressed at my handling at first base. I was relieved that I could still do it. I needed the batting practice that displayed my rusty swing, but I worked out the kinks, although my body yelled at me that night. I was, after all, quite a bit older, and while in good condition, here I was playing on a team with twentysomethings. The game was great fun, the other team didn't much like me, the Kyodo Tokyo's very tall gaijin (foreign white man), their secret weapon. The game was full of intense competition, and I did hit a run-scoring double. Our team won, and after lining up with the other team for bows and handshakes, Spike came out from our van with a case of beer. Seems, in Japan, the winning team supplies the beer.

BAMBOO FLUTE

While in Japan, I was hoping to find a traditional bamboo flute, a shakuhachi, and phoned Spike to ask if he would inquire about it. He phoned back, said that he found a master flute maker, that he made an appointment for us to visit his shop, and to meet him and the "boys" downstairs at two o'clock. The boys wanted to tag along in the van and be my entourage. Off we went and arrived at the flute maker's shop after a ride filled with them laughing and cracking jokes. I had no idea what was so funny, and Spike was not forthcoming. He just said, "Japanese jokes cannot be translated." I left it alone.

I was introduced to the master craftsman. He was curious about a gaijin wanting a shakuhachi, and speaking through Spike, told me that the instrument, when played well, brought forth the voice of the soul. He hoped I would honor this, and I told him that I was sincere in my respect for the instrument. He showed me various levels of instruments, from a student model on up, and then presented an instrument that he said was one of his finest and thought I should have it. It was made from the root section of the bamboo plant, and had lain in the forest for many years, which gave it its unique tone. I played a few passages on it and was amazed by its sound. I was sold.

The man cautioned me that in taking it from its natural environment, it could split, and I would have to be very careful as to how it was repaired. I assured him I would care for it. I paid him quite a large sum in yen. I don't remember exactly, but today these master instruments range from three thousand dollars on up. As I gave my formal goodbye, the man put a used student flute in my hand and said that it was a gift for me to practice on and was not as delicate as my fine purchase.

We left the shop, and I was very pleased with my new instrument. On the way back to the hotel, the guys were at it again, laughing back and forth.

I said, "Spike, enough, what's going on with all the back-and-forth?"

He said, "Okay, here's what is going on. The boys want to know why you need another shakuhachi. Is the one you have not working well for you? Do the girls complain?"

"Oh c'mon, wait a minute," I said, "are they talking about . . . ?"

"Yes," Spike said, "we boys today make fun of some of our elders' customs. We do not mean disrespect, but in our world, we say shakuhachi when talking about a penis. So, they laugh at your needing another shakuhachi, and now you have three. Please do not take offense. It's all in fun."

I looked back at them, and with a grin, I said, "Looks like you guys are in a shakuhachi band." We all had a good laugh.

MELBOURNE, AUSTRALIA:
NINA SIMONE MEETS THE ABORIGINAL WOMEN'S GROUP

JAPAN / AUSTRALIA TOUR

November 1973

THE MELBOURNE CONCERT was a wild and woolly affair. It started with a press conference the day before, where Nina threatened to quit if photos taken were published that showed her trying to strangle the notorious journalist, "Bob the Beast," who was rude and asked her unflattering questions. It was eventually handled by an Australian Journalists Association official, who was there and reprimanded the reporter. They managed to kill the photos, *but look out, Al,* Nina was really on edge.

True to form, the next day, Michael Deane, the partner of our promoter, Lew Kidd, told me that hotel reception had phoned, complaining that a guest told them they'd seen a Black woman at the swimming pool the night before dropping her dress and diving in naked. Of course, that wasn't unusual to me, but . . .

At the concert, we had a full house. We were twenty minutes into the show when something ticked off Nina. She left the stage with me quickly behind her thinking, *now what?* After a few minutes, Lew pushed Michael out onstage to make up some excuse, and I finally persuaded Nina to return. She went out, and as she passed the mic stand, she kicked it over. Michael ran out, and, as he told it to me, "As I bent over to pick up the stand, I felt this presence behind me and I thought I was being stabbed in the back, and I jumped. It was Nina running her finger up my spine, and I nearly shit my pants." The audience was laughing.

Nina was still uptight and started singing "Young, Gifted, and Black." Then someone in the audience shouted, "and Gay," wherein Nina's eyes lit up, and that's when she got into the concert. A bunch of kids ran down the aisle to the stage, and Lew and Michael had to keep them off. From that point on, the evening was amazing, other than the theater manager turning the houselights up at midnight in the middle of a number. Michael had to run to his office and tell him to turn them back off, as Nina was not finished. She stayed on for almost an hour longer. It was certainly a wonderful and memorable evening.

We were going to enjoy a couple of days off before moving on to Sydney, and I was relaxing in the lounge of the Old Melbourne Inn with Nina, having a cocktail. I had been telling Nina that I was invited to play a round of golf with one of the tour publicists when a group of Aboriginal women appeared and stood before us. One of the ladies, the spokesperson, introduced themselves as the Council for Aboriginal Women of South Australia. They were having a conference in the hotel, had attended Nina's concert, were devoted fans, and hoped Nina might speak to the group. Nina angrily said that she was relaxing after working so hard the night before, and that they were big girls and should be able to take care of themselves.

I sat there and said, "Wait a minute, Nina. Don't go off on these ladies. They admire you."

Nina turned to me and yelled, "I ain't their mother."

"Oh, yes, you are," I said firmly back to her.

She looked at me and said demurely, "Okay, I guess you're right. Where and when is this meeting?" she said to the women.

"Right now in the conference hall."

Nina laughed and said, "You don't waste any time. C'mon, Al, let's go." She got up and said to the ladies, "Lead the way."

We entered the hall, and there were at least a hundred women, who upon seeing Nina stood up and applauded. I remained in the back as Nina was led up to the stage, while the women were still applauding and yelling, "Nina, Nina." She grabbed the microphone and with a smile on her face said, "We women have the same problem everywhere in the world, especially women of color. We're fighting the government, we're fighting white folks, AND we're fighting our men, who are useless." She was building up a head of steam, and I hoped she wouldn't go off on us. Then Nina laughed, calmed down, and said, "What I mean to say, is that it is the responsibility of women to stand up for their rights and not rely on the goodness of politicians to change their ways. You have to demand your rights and keep your demands in their faces. Swamp them with mail, demonstrate, let 'em know you ain't goin' away. Listen to Bob Marley, you know who I mean? Learn his song and keep singin' it, make it your anthem." Without warning, Nina burst out singing, "Get up, stand up, stand up for your rights." She got the crowd singing with her. Many of them knew the song. Some didn't, but got carried along in the enthusiasm.

Nina finished by saying she was proud of them. Saying, "Stay strong," and "I wanna read about y'all raisin' hell in the newspapers when I'm back home." The women roared, chanting "NI-NA, NI-NA," over and over while I ran up and got her out of there.

She looked at me and said, "You happy now? Back to the lounge. I need a drink."

We sat down on a big old leather sofa, and I said to her, "Nina, that was as good as Stokely and Malcom."

She laughed and said, "Where do you think I got all that shit from? And you know Marley wrote that song last year when he visited Haiti and saw what was goin' on. Civil rights is worldwide now."

"No, Mama," I said, "that wasn't Stokely and Malcolm, you were on fire. That was you."

She said, "Oh, I suppose you're right, Al."

FODDER ON HER WINGS

ONE NIGHT ON TOUR.

This is the beginning of Nina's original song, "Fodder on Her Wings."

> "A bird fell to earth, reincarnated from her birth,
> She had fodder in her brain,
> Dust inside her wings
> Oh how sad, oh how sad . . . ."

Nina was in a melancholy mood that night, pensive and distant, standing offstage about to go on. She turned and said, "I'll do this alone," and walked to the piano under the applause from a capacity audience.

Nina waited until the hall quieted and began a rumbling movement in the lower register of the piano. She gradually moved the sound upward with her left hand and continued that sound as she began a melodic, ghost-like movement that sounded like the spirit of Vladimir Rachmaninoff. She kept building on her theme, the melody of "Fodder on Her Wings," becoming more powerful and stormy as she went along. She was possessed by something moving through her. I'm sure she had no idea, at that point, that she was in front of an audience. On and on she went, building and building her structure, at times humming guttural sounds to herself, creating variations, bringing images of Bach and Chopin into the tapestry that she was weaving. Nothing planned. This was pure improvisation.

She went on for at least fifteen minutes and suddenly at the height of a crescendo she stopped, and with her notes still reverberating in the hall, she laid down a quiet chord and began to sing, "A bird fell to earth . . ." Her song depicts an innocent soul, in the form of a bird, who came to this earth reincarnated with the detritus of humanity on her wings and her spirit, and with dust and dirt tainting her brain. She tells how the bird moved throughout the world, watching how people live, forgetting to give and care for one another. She ended the song softly singing, "Oh how sad, Oh how sad."

The audience was totally captured, and how lucky they were to be in the presence of this incredible performance. Pure genius, a once in a lifetime moment.

Nina ended the song with her signature wild dissonant arpeggios, fingers blazing across the entire keyboard, a cacophony of sound. And then she just stopped, sat there a moment, and as the audience went wild with applause, got up, and without acknowledging the ovation, walked off the stage, reached out her hand to me, and, visibly shaken, said, "I'm done, Al, take me to my dressing room."

Her whole performance lasted maybe twenty-five minutes, and after sitting in the hall for a while without Nina returning, the audience started clapping in unison and started yelling, "Ni-na, Ni-na." They were expecting an evening's performance of perhaps an hour and a half, and felt shortchanged, forgetting the incredible piece of music that they had just experienced.

In her dressing room, Nina had sunk down in an easy

chair. I poured her a glass of champagne. She looked up at me, and still shaken, said, "I don't know where I went, Al, but I know that it must have been somethin'."

The promoter barged into the room and said, "Nina, the crowd is very upset. Please, you have to go out there andplay."

Nina just sat there, glared up at him and said, "Listen, mutha fucka, if they didn't appreciate what they just got, they can all go to hell. You can go out there and tell them that for me."

Indeed, the house lights went up, the promoter went out and apologized and said that Nina had become ill and could not continue.

Maybe the people that didn't "get it" are also those who visited the Louvre to view the Mona Lisa and were disappointed to find that the painting was "so small."

I hoped this rare moment in music was not lost on at least some of the people in the audience that night. They were in the presence of genius.

EXCERPT FROM LETTER FROM NINA SIMONE

June 6, 1977

Dearest Al - Sweet Sweet Thing -

... I miss you...so much more than I can say... in fact, I cried so long and hard when we were taking off that it felt a little like dying. It is incredible - the levels of feeling. I sound so analytical But BELIEVE ME I FELT IT SO DEEPLY I thought the tears would never stop. I love you so...

... I love you very much...I have your beautiful picture from the bulletin board. I stole it. It is framed already. Must work now so I won't feel depressed.

... my Home is as beautiful as ever and my "air" is FRESH & Clean. My Mountains speak of love of beauty.

Love you madly,

Nina

CODA

OUR FAREWELL Nina Simone tour opened on June 8, 2001, at the Palais des Congrés de Paris. The band consisted of Paul Robinson on drums, Tony Jones on bass, Leopoldo Fleming on percussion, and me on guitar. This band had been with Nina since the 1980s, all of us completely dedicated to Nina. In a band, we know the drummer's role, among other things, is to keep the beat, and add dynamics. Paul not only played that role, he played NINA, totally in touch with her every nuance. Such was our band of brothers.

Nina and I stood offstage together, holding hands as we always did, ready to go on after the introduction. She turned to me and softly said, "This is all we have, Al, isn't it. This is our life, and everything else comes after this." I felt that Nina was saying this, not with sadness but with acceptance of her journey, as reflected in her song, "My Way."

Frail, voice unsteady, and a shadow of her vibrant, explosive past, Nina entered the stage, and was overwhelmed by a tumultuous, standing ovation. She stood by her piano, bowed to the audience. The cheers were deafening. She sat down, reached out toward her loving fans, and with a warm smile said, "Hello, it's so good to be here with you again. I hope you missed me.

HANDWRITTEN LETTER FROM NINA

June 6 1977
9:30 A.M.
At Home

DEAREST AL - SWEET SWEET THING -
I HAVE BEEN IN my HOUSE only TEN
minutes & it is delightful To Be BACK
EXCEPT I miss YOU, Mimi (WHO MET US IN N.Y)
& LISA & DOROTHEA (WHOM I CALLED While I WAS
THERE) SO much more THAN I CAN SAY.
IN FACT, I CRIED SO Long & HARD WHEN
we were TAKING OFF THAT IT FELT A LITTLE
Like Dying. IT is INCREDIBLE — the levels
of feeling. I sound so ANALYTICAL BUT
BELIEVE ME I FELT IT SO DEEPLY I Thought
The TEARS WOULD NEVER STOP. I LOVE you so,
AND I miss ALL my FRIENDS. Mike's NOT
coming with us WAS Also A Blow. But
who KNOWS; perhaps he is feeling the same
way. Perhaps you are TOO. I knew I couldn't
STAY - I REALLY HAD BEGUN TO go BANANAS.
But TO come home without my HUSBAND
here (who ever that is) Still HURTS. But
NOT TO WORRY. I'm Fine. Now that I
CAN THINK, it ~~occurs~~ ocurrs To me that there
WAS A WAY I could have stayed AT
MACS. IT Didn't hit me (& Apparently No
one else) to ASK How Long it would have
TAKEN TO Fix the WATER OR if it would
Have BEEN possible To Live with only
one Bath - or whatever. Point is: There
WAS A way to stay (I THINK) But I couldn't
Think! That's Exactly it. That's the problem for me IN
N.Y. plus no sleep.

Concerts scaring me now. Because of Lack of Co ordinated practice & whatever. This thing is between <u>you</u> & <u>me</u>. Will practice more BRECHT.

Am still moving with much Energy. I am tired But content. But will do many things today <u>before</u> I completely relax tonight or tomorrow. When that happens, one <u>goes</u> <u>to sleep</u> (Smiles).

First thing is to Frame my Doctorate! Bravo! <u>This</u> morning I am doing it.

Gene wanted to stay in N.Y. <u>Alone</u>. Mimi didn't <u>want</u> <u>her</u> (it's that simple) But of cource I couldn't let her. But she is happy is thirsty now very much for <u>NEW</u> <u>YORK</u>.

Would like to write Mac or <u>you</u> ask him if it's possible to be his guests <u>AGAIN</u> from ~~June~~ 26 through the 4th!

If it is awkward I'll write him. I only have his number - no address - I gladly write him. I'm losing <u>too</u> <u>much</u> <u>money</u>. It costs $500 more to come home 2nd class! But trip was on 747 & I slept all the way. & it was comfortable.

I Hope you get man from Fabergé & I'll write Teddy . . .

WRITE. I love you very
much.

I have you Beautiful picture
from the Bulletin BOARD. I STOLE it
It is FRAMED AlREADY. MUST WORK NOW.
SO I won't feel DEPRESSED.

My Home is AS BEAUTIFUL AS
ever And my "AIR" is FRESH & CleAN.
& My MOUNTAINS speaks of Love of
BEAUTY. Love you MADLY..

P.S. Will sleep with The "idiot"
PAUL Tonight SO I won't
BE Lonely.

Mia

ACKNOWLEDGMENTS

To all my friends who listened to my tales of adventure and encouraged me to move forward in creating this book, I am grateful and embrace you with profound thanks. This endeavor was not without angst, and your support was the wheels that rolled me along.

I would particularly like to thank:

Joe Sorce, who lent me his ear and gave me sage advice.

Candy Christmas, who cracked the whip, and kept telling me the book would come to be.

Marcia Leonard, for giving me my first real ray of hope.

My daughter, Davi Weston, for solving all my picky problems.

Tom Ingling, for his computer brilliance.

Dan Armstrong, for his painstaking research.

Roger Nupie, faithful keeper of Nina Simone archives.

Ginny, you polished my rambling stories into a meaningful and insightful tale of my life's adventures. It never would have reached fruition without your guidance. As I show in this book, my life just happened to me, and along my journey, there were, and are, fantastic people who contributed to my growth, sat together in musical friendship, taught me to listen, and pushed me further in my life than I ever dreamed.

Among them:

Rector Bailey, Garry Sherman, Robert Henry, Wynton Kelly, Bob Dorough, Rudy Guarnaccia (Big Rudy), Leopoldo Fleming, Chris White, Laurena White, Paul Robinson, William Eaton, Ron Carter, Duke Pearson, Bruce Langhorne, John Switzer, Maynard Silva, Ram Ramirez, Steve and Joyce Maxner, Jeremy Berlin, Basia Jaworska, Nick Branch, Dan Waters, Bob Branaman, Chris Skellenger, Patrick Niemisto, Dr. Edward Harrington, Kevin Zoernig, Scott MacMillan and Brian Doyle.

In memory of Yvonne Roehler, builder of beautiful books.

NOTABLE PEOPLE

AHMED ABDUL-MALIK (1927–1993) American jazz double bassist and oud player.

PEPPER ADAMS (1930–1986) American jazz baritone saxophonist and composer.

SAM ASH (1897–1956) Violinist, teacher, and entrepreneur who founded the Sam Ash Music Stores.

NNAMDI AZIKIWE (1904–1996) Known as Zik of Africa, Azikiwe was a Nigerian politician and revolutionary leader.

JAMES BALDWIN (1924–1987) Writer and civil rights activist acclaimed for his essays, novels, plays, and poems.

GEORGE BARRIE (1912–2002) Creator of the men's cologne Brut, movie producer, and songwriter whose songs received two Oscar nominations.

BELLE BARTH (1911–1971) Jewish-American comedian working in the 1950s and 1960s.

HARRY BELAFONTE (1927–2023) American singer, actor, and civil rights activist, who popularized calypso music with international audiences in the 1950s and 1960s.

BOBBY BENSON (1922–1983) Entertainer and musician who influenced Nigerian music, introducing big band and Caribbean idioms to the highlife style of West African music.

LEONARD BERNSTEIN (1918–1990) Conductor, composer, pianist, music educator, and author.

THEODORE BIKEL (1924–2015) Austrian-American actor, singer, musician, composer, unionist, and political activist.

BERTOLT BRECHT (1898–1956) German theatre practitioner, playwright, and poet.

OSCAR BROWN, JR. (1926–2005) American singer, songwriter, playwright, poet, actor, and civil rights activist.

DAVE BRUBECK (1920–2012) American jazz pianist and composer.

LENNY BRUCE (1925–1966) American stand-up comedian, social critic, and satirist.

SOLOMON BURKE (1940–2010) American singer who shaped the sound of R&B as one of the founding fathers of soul music in the 1960s.

BILLY BYERS (1927–1996) American jazz trombonist and arranger.

SAMMY CAHN (1913–1993) American lyricist, songwriter, and musician.

GEORGE CARLIN (1937–2008) American stand-up comedian, social critic, actor, and author.

RON CARTER (1937–) American jazz double bassist.

RAY CHARLES (1930–2004) American singer, songwriter, and pianist.

CHARLIE CHRISTIAN (1916–1942) American swing and jazz guitarist.

CHARLES HONI COLES (1911–1992) American actor and tap dancer.

WALTER CRONKITE (1916–2009) Anchor for the CBS Evening News from 1962 to 1981.

TADD DAMERON (1917–1965) American jazz composer, arranger, and pianist.

MILES DAVIS (1926–1991) American jazz trumpeter, bandleader, and composer.

SAMMY DAVIS JR. (1925–1990) American singer, actor, comedian, dancer, and musician.

PAUL DESMOND (1924–1977) Jazz alto saxophonist, composer, and proponent of cool jazz.

ART D'LUGOFF (1924–2009) American jazz impresario.

BOB DOROUGH (1923–2018) American bebop and cool jazz vocalist, pianist, and composer.

TOM DOWD (1925–2002) Recording engineer and producer for Atlantic Records.

BOB DYLAN (1941–) American singer-songwriter.

AHMET ERTEGUN (1923-2006) music producer, co-founder of Atlantic Records.

NESUHI ERTEGUN (1917-1989) music producer, co-founder of Atlantic Records.

BOOKER ERVIN (1930–1970) American tenor saxophonist.

LEOPOLDO FLEMING (1939–2025) Percussionist, composer, arranger, and musical director who accompanied Miriam Makeba and Nina Simone.

PETER FONDA (1940–2019) American actor, film director, and screenwriter.

LUKAS FOSS (1922–2009) German-American composer, pianist, and conductor.

FRANK FOSTER (1928–2011) Tenor and soprano saxophonist, flautist, arranger, and composer.

ARETHA FRANKLIN (1942–2018) American singer, song-writer, and pianist.

CHARLES GANIMIAN (1926–1988) Armenian-American musician and singer known for his virtuosity on the oud.

JERRY GARCIA (1942–1995) Lead guitarist and a vocalist for the Grateful Dead.

JAMES GARNER (1928–2014) American actor.

GEORGE GERSHWIN (1898–1937) Composer and pianist spanning jazz, popular, and classical music.

DIZZY GILLESPIE (1917–1993) Jazz trumpeter, bandleader, composer, educator, and singer.

MAX GORDON (1903–1989) Jazz promoter, founder of the Village Vanguard in New York City.

ALBERT GROSSMAN (1926–1986) Entrepreneur and promoter of folk music and rock and roll.

ALEX HALEY (1921–1992) Writer and the author of the 1976 bestseller *Roots*.

BOBBY HAMILTON (1935–2019) Jazz drummer

LORRAINE HANSBERRY (1930–1965) American playwright and writer.

JOHNNY HARTMAN (1923–1983) Jazz singer known for his rich baritone ballads.

RICHIE HAVENS (1941–2013) American singer-songwriter and guitarist.

STERLING HAYDEN (1916–1986) American actor, author, sailor, and Marine.

MILT HINTON (1910–2000) American double bassist and photographer.

BILLIE HOLIDAY (1915–1959) American singer of swing music and jazz.

LANGSTON HUGHES (1901–1967) Poet, activist, novelist, and playwright from Joplin, Missouri.

AHMAD JAMAl (1930–2023) American jazz pianist, composer, bandleader, and educator.

J. J. JOHNSON (1924–2001) American jazz trombonist, composer, and arranger.

QUINCY JONES (1933–2024) Producer, composer, conductor, trumpeter, and bandleader.

GRACE KELLY (1929–1982) American actress and Princess of Monaco from 1956 to 1982.

WYNTON KELLY (1931–1971) American jazz pianist and composer.

BEN E. KING (1938–2015) American soul and R&B singer and songwriter.

BRUCE LANGHORNE (1938–2017) American folk guitarist and session musician who shaped the birth of folk-rock, accompanying Bob Dylan on his early recordings.

NORMAN LEAR (1922–2023) Screenwriter and producer who wrote, created or developed over 100 TV shows.

MICHEL LEGRAND (1932–2019) French composer, arranger, jazz pianist, and singer.

VIOLA LIUZZO (1925–1965) American civil rights activist from Detroit, Michigan.

MOMS MABLEY (1897–1975) American stand-up comedian and actress.

RALPH MACDONALD (1944–2011) Percussionist, songwriter, arranger, and producer.

JOHNNY MANDEL (1925–2020) American composer of popular songs, film music, and jazz.

BOB MARLEY (1945–1981) Jamaican singer, songwriter, and guitarist.

ROGER MCGUINN (1942–) American folk-rock musician best known as leader of The Byrds.

PRINCESS LALLA MERYEM (1962–) Daughter and eldest child of King Hassan II of Morocco.

HENRY MILLER (1891–1980) American novelist, short-story writer, and essayist.

THELONIOUS MONK (1917–1982) American jazz pianist and composer.

JAMES MOODY (1925–2010) Jazz saxophonist and flute player and occasional vocalist who played in the bebop style.

JAMIL NASSER (1932–2010) American jazz musician.

BARRY NEWMAN (1930–2023) American actor of stage, screen, and television.

KIM NOVAK (1933–) American retired actress and painter.

VICTOR OLAIYA (1930–2020) Nigerian trumpeter who played in the highlife style.

BABATUNDE OLATUNJI (1927–2003) Nigerian drummer, educator, and social activist.

CHARLIE PARKER (1920–1955) Nicknamed "Bird" Parker was an American jazz saxophonist, bandleader and composer.

DUKE PEARSON (1932–1980) American jazz pianist and composer.

BROCK PETERS (1927–2005) Actor known for roles in *Porgy & Bess* and *To Kill a Mockingbird.*

OSCAR PETERSON (1925–2007) Canadian jazz pianist and composer.

GEORGE PLIMPTON (1927–2003) Writer known for his participatory journalism and founder of *The Paris Review.*

SIDNEY POITIER (1927–2022) Bahamian-American actor, film director, activist, and diplomat.

SERGEI RACHMANINOFF (1873–1943) Russian composer, virtuoso pianist, and conductor.

RAM RAMIREZ (1913–1994) Puerto Rican jazz pianist and composer.

JAMES REEB (1927–1965) Pastor and activist in the American civil rights movement.

DJANGO REINHARDT (1910–1953) Belgian-born Romani jazz guitarist and composer in France.

BEN RILEY (1933–2017) Jazz drummer known for his work with Thelonious Monk and the group Sphere.

PAUL ROBESON (1898–1976) American baritone, actor, football player, and activist famous for his cultural accomplishments and political stances.

NEIL SEDAKA (1939–) American singer, songwriter, and pianist.

ANDRES SEGOVIA (1893–1987) Spanish virtuoso classical guitarist.

BROTHER JOHN SELLERS (1924–1999) American gospel and folk singer.

PETER SELLERS (1925–1980) English actor and comedian.

RAVI SHANKAR (1920–2012) Indian sitarist and composer.

GARRY SHERMAN (1933–) Award-winning musician and producer, composing film soundtracks for *Midnight Cowboy, The Heartbreak Kid* and underscoring for *Alice's Restaurant*.

SIMONE SIGNORET (1921–1985) French actress and Oscar winner (Room at the Top, 1959).

NINA SIMONE (1933–2003) American singer, pianist, songwriter, and civil rights activist.

SONNY STITT (1924–1982) American jazz saxophonist of the bebop/hard bop idiom.

MARY TRAVERS (1936–2009) Member of the 1960s folk trio Peter, Paul and Mary.

SARAH VAUGHAN (1924–1990) American jazz singer and pianist.

RAY WALSTON (1914–2001) American actor famous for his role in *My Favorite Martian*.

DIONNE WARWICK (1940–) American singer, actress, and television host.

DINAH WASHINGTON (1924–1963) American singer and pianist popular in the 1950s.

KURT WEILL (1900–1950) German-born composer who fled the Nazis for Broadway and Hollywood.

GEORGE WEIN (1925–2021) American jazz promoter, pianist, and producer.

RANDY WESTON (1926–2018) American jazz pianist and composer.

CHRIS WHITE (1936–2014) Chris White was an American jazz bassist.

JOSH WHITE (1914–1969) Singer, guitarist, songwriter, actor, and civil rights activist.

JOE WILLIAMS (1918–1999) American jazz and blues singer.

PHIL WOODs (1931–2015) Jazz alto saxophonist, clarinetist, bandleader, and composer.

ANDREW YOUNG (1932–) American politician, diplomat, and civil rights leader.

FARON YOUNG (1932–1996) American country singer, musician, and songwriter.

GEORGE YOUNG (1937–) American jazz saxophonist.

HENNY YOUNGMAN (1906–1998) English-born comedian and musician.